PERFECT STRANGERS

PERFECT STRANGERS

A Story of Love, Strength, and Recovery
After the Boston Marathon Bombing

ROSEANN SDOIA

with Jennifer Jordan

BBS

PUBLICAFFAIRS
New York

PublicAffairs
Hachette Book Group
1290 Avenue of the Americas, New York, NY 10104
www.publicaffairsbooks.com
@Public_Affairs

Printed in the United States of America
Originally published in hardcover and ebook by PublicAffairs in March 2017
First Trade Paperback Edition: April 2019

Published by PublicAffairs, an imprint of Perseus Books, LLC, a subsidiary of Hachette Book Group, Inc. The PublicAffairs name and logo is a trademark of the Hachette Book Group.

The Hachette Speakers Bureau provides a wide range of authors for speaking events. To find out more, go to www.hachettespeakersbureau.com or call (866) 376-6591.

The publisher is not responsible for websites (or their content) that are not owned by the publisher.

Book Interior Design by Jeff Williams

The Library of Congress has cataloged the hardcover edition as follows:

Names: Sdoia, Roseann, author.
Title: Perfect strangers : friendship, strength, and recovery after Boston's worst day / Roseann Sdoia.
Description: New York : PublicAffairs, 2017.
Identifiers: LCCN 2016047561 (print) | LCCN 2017002348 (ebook) | ISBN 9781610397001 (hardcover) | ISBN 9781610397018 (ebook)
Subjects: LCSH: Sdoia, Roseann. | Boston Marathon Bombing, Boston, Mass., 2013. | Victims of terrorism—Massachusetts—Boston—Biography. | Terrorism—Social aspects—Massachusetts—Boston.
Classification: LCC HV6432.8 .S395 2017 (print) | LCC HV6432.8 (ebook) | DDC 363.325/97964252092 [B] —dc23
LC record available at https://lccn.loc.gov/2016047561

ISBNs: 978-1-61039-700-1 (hardcover); 978-1-61039-701-8 (ebook); 978-1-5417-7404-9 (paperback)

LSC-C

10 9 8 7 6 5 4 3 2 1

This book is dedicated to all of those who
have been touched by terrorist actions and to
the memory of those whose lives have been lost.

CONTENTS

TWO YEARS LATER

ON APRIL 15, 2013, a dark line was drawn through the middle of my life. Before that day, I was a single professional woman living in the North End of Boston. I vacationed in Europe, skied at Sunday River and Killington, ran 5- and 10K fun runs with my friends, and spent most summer weekends on Nantucket or in Newport, Rhode Island. That was the life in which I had two legs.

On that day, I found myself on the other side of that line, half sitting, half lying on the sidewalk. After a few dazed moments, my eyes began to focus and found the pool of blood gathering underneath me and dripping off the curb onto Boylston Street. That was the day of the Boston Marathon bombing, which killed 3 people and injured 264 others. It was also the day that I lost my right leg.

••••••

Two years later, almost to the day, I found myself sitting in a modest living room in a working-class neighborhood in Boston, eating a piece of gluten-free pizza, sipping red wine, and looking across the table at three people whose lives had also been irrevocably changed that day and who are now as familiar and as dear to me as those I've known my whole life.

I'm not sure exactly when it was that we became a family—Boston police officer Shana Cottone, firefighter Mike Materia, Northeastern University student Shores Salter, and I. All I know is that we shared an experience that has left each of us forever changed. And while most people who were there that day remember it with only horror, outrage, and sorrow, we four can now also see it through the lens of the love and support that formed in the wake of that atrocity.

That night, over pizza and wine, we did something we rarely do. We compared notes about that day—what we remembered of the bombing and its immediate aftermath.

"I remember thinking you had the whitest teeth I'd ever seen," Shana told me, and we all laughed. Shana has since quit, but at the time she chewed tobacco, and the color of her teeth showed it.

"I remember you asking if we were taking Storrow Drive to Mass General, and I was like, 'Wow, lady, let the driver drive,'" Mike said. "I couldn't believe you were backseat driving even with your leg blown off!"

We all laughed because Mike knows what a terrible backseat driver I am. He reached over and lightly touched my left leg where it rested against his on the couch. That simple gesture has brought me more comfort and reassurance than I would ever have thought possible.

"I remember you saying, 'I don't think I have my leg,'" Shores said, "and my heart absolutely sank to the bottom of my stomach." Quick tears came to his eyes. I reached across the coffee table and held on to his arm.

"I'll never forget that," he added quietly, his head down and slowly shaking back and forth.

"And I remember feeling, for one quick instant, as I lay on the pavement looking up at the faces hovering over me, like Dorothy in *The Wizard of Oz*: here are the three people who will get me back alive—my Scarecrow, Lion, and Tin Man." That's what I remember.

······

Would I like my leg back? Of course.

Does Shana wish her patrol of the barricades along Boylston Street had involved the typical routine of boisterous college kids and woozy runners? Obviously.

Mike wishes he hadn't had to transport a bloodied and shell-shocked victim to the hospital in the back of a police paddy wagon, holding her hand and telling her she wasn't going to die.

And Shores wishes the most memorable moments of his sophomore year in college were acing his exams and spring break in San Diego, not the traumatic events of that day.

But none of us would trade what we've gained for what we've lost. Shana, Shores, Mike, and I are all grateful for what we've found in each other. Our lives are filled with more joy, fun, and love than we could have believed.

I am not just telling my story. I am telling our story—each of the people who was on the front line, literally, in saving my life—my three wonderful new friends as well as the doctors, nurses, police officers, firefighters, coworkers, and a few of my oldest and dearest friends who were there with me watching the marathon that day and whose love and bravery inspire me constantly. I quite literally wouldn't be here without them.

And this is a story about my favorite day in my favorite city in the world and how, in an instant, that day went from being pure celebration to desperate survival. For those of us who made it off the sidewalk that horrific day, and those who made sure we did, this book is about taking back our favorite day while never forgetting those who were lost.

chapter one

VERTICALLY CHALLENGED

WE BOSTONIANS LOOK forward to Marathon Monday like no other day. Not only is it the unofficial beginning of spring, but it's also always held on the third Monday of April—Patriots' Day—a state holiday that commemorates Paul Revere's legendary midnight ride from Boston to Lexington and the first bloodshed of the Revolutionary War. For those who don't want to spend the entire day at a twenty-six-mile-long street party, there's the Boston Red Sox game at Fenway. The first pitch is early, 11:00 a.m., so that by the end of the ninth inning fans can walk to nearby Kenmore Square and catch the runners coming through their last mile on their way to the finish.

For many native Bostonians, Marathon Monday is a tradition. It certainly was in my family. It was a tradition for my father, my sister, Gia, and me to drive into Boston together that morning. And it was a tradition for Mom to stay home: for her, the idea of running for any reason other than escaping a fire is simply ridiculous. So Gia, Dad, and I would drive the forty-five minutes from Dracut, Massachusetts, into Boston. Because Dad was never much of a map reader, we'd always end up on the Cambridge side of the Charles River and have to pull a U-ie back over the river and into the city before finding a parking lot near Fenway Park. Once there, we'd eat our fill of ballpark franks and popcorn before leaving the park early and making our way through the crowded streets to watch the runners come through Kenmore Square.

••••••

The first man known to have run the marathon distance of twenty-six miles dropped dead soon after. In 490 BC, a Greek soldier named Pheidippides ran from Marathon to Athens to announce that the Greeks had won their war with the Persians. While nothing could match that sort of legendary origin, the Boston Marathon is nonetheless America's oldest foot race and over its 120-year history has no shortage of legends who have crossed the famed yellow finish line, from Clarence DeMar's record seven wins to Johnny Kelley's record sixty-one finishes—more than any runner in any race history—to the inglorious Rosie Ruiz, who in 1980 hopped into the race only a few blocks from the finish and was erroneously awarded the crown (a crown she has yet to return, by the way). But beyond the folklore, the Boston Marathon is perhaps most coveted by runners because of the crowds. From the start in Hopkinton to the finish 26.2 miles later in downtown Boston, massive crowds line the entire course. And they don't merely watch. They scream; they yell; they hold up hilarious signs to keep the spirits of the runners high; they run alongside offering water or orange slices; they blow whistles and bells. All day long, and to thousands of complete strangers running for the finish, Boston gives everything it's got. It's a remarkable outpouring of love and respect and encouragement, and runners come from all over the world to experience its magic.

Marathon Monday, April 15, 2013, began as it had for the previous 117 years. You couldn't have asked for a better day to run 26.2 miles—cool and crisp, with a light breeze out of the west at the runners' backs, helping to push them (perhaps mentally if not physically) toward the finish in Boston. The year before, the temperatures had hovered around a dangerous 95 degrees, and officials had almost canceled the entire race. In the end, the race had been run, but after race directors had offered a rain check for the following year, 2,200 entrants had opted to wait and run in 2013 under "safer" conditions. Before dawn the city came alive, with over 23,000 anxious runners making their way by car or bus to the race start in Hopkinton. The trip back to Boston would be made under their own steam. Thousands of police officers from Hopkinton to Boston attended roll call in their local station houses, getting their assignments for the day, most of them positioned somewhere along the perimeter of the race. Their primary duty would be keeping the estimated one million spectators on the sidewalk side of the barricades and out of the way of the passing runners in the streets. Hundreds of firefighters and EMTs had strategically parked their fire trucks and ambulances along the route for those needing emergency care. During every race, they were needed to address a laundry list of runners' ailments—heatstroke, dehydration, muscle cramps, shin splints, and gastrointestinal distress were the usual culprits that brought runners to their knees and out of the race.

That morning I woke up feeling a satisfying fatigue in my legs from having run the Boston Athletic Association's 5K Fun Run the day before. Running it had been a goal of mine for years, but because it took place early on a Sunday morning and I and most of my girlfriends usually chose to sleep in and then gather for brunch around 10:00 a.m., I'd never made it. But that year I decided to forgo the brunch. I ran the 5K, and I absolutely loved it. The best thing about the race is that it takes you across the finish line on the Boston Marathon course. Even though it's the day before and you're not running the actual marathon, the thrill of watching your feet cross that iconic yellow line is truly thrilling. I am not known for emotional outbursts, yet even I teared up. Every year, watching the runners go by, I'd think about training for and running the marathon, but this year I felt inspired in a way that I never had before. As I walked over to meet my friends after the race, I promised myself that I would tackle the full marathon someday.

As a girl, I'd been quite the athlete. I was always in motion—cartwheeling across lawns; playing softball; and running, flipping, and spinning through gymnastics classes. Even my hands were busy. When I learned sign language in junior high, I spent months driving my mother to distraction by signing every word that was spoken in my presence, including my own name. But then puberty hit, and with it a few extra pounds and breasts that overwhelmed my tiny five-foot-one-inch frame. All of a sudden, my body felt out of balance. Then came high school, and my athletic pursuits were replaced by friends, boyfriends, and beer. I would never again call myself athletic. Active, yes, but athletic? Not so much. As an adult, I became more of a "morning-after" runner. You know the kind. We're the ones who gather at our favorite bars with our favorite friends on Friday and Saturday nights, eat too much of the wrong food, have *just one more* before heading home, and then try to run it all off in the morning.

Unlike millions of marathoners around the world, I did *not* experience that wondrous beta-endorphin high after a long run, probably because I ran three miles at a time, not thirteen. I had a complicated relationship with running: I would grumble, forcing myself out the door for a run, and then absolutely love how I felt after I had done it. I would feel pride and accomplishment from pushing myself even a little outside my comfort zone. Try as I would to push myself past the five-mile mark on a regular basis, I managed to run seven miles only a couple of times.

But what brings me out to the sidelines every year, and what brings out so many Bostonians and others, is that we can tap in to some of that amazing energy just by being there—being a part of the energy that keeps those runners going. It's one of the reasons why Marathon Monday is a celebration for all—runners and spectators alike. Just being in that wave of joy is intoxicating; its power overwhelms even the most committed couch potato. We absorb the runners' excitement, see the simple and, yes, tortured pride on their faces, knowing that behind them is twenty-six miles and before them at the finish is a rare moment in life: pure euphoria at having accomplished something monumental.

It was a postcard-perfect New England spring day—a navy-blue sky, the first lilac and magnolia-blossom buds making the trees shimmer a verdant green, and the softest of breezes filling the crowded North End streets around my apartment with fresh sea air. The winter had been a long one (another tradition in Boston), so when I opened my eyes to the day, I couldn't wait to meet it. I had a fabulous day planned. First I would attend the Red Sox game with my friend Sabrina, and while we watched, we'd be able to monitor our friend Jen's race progress on the official marathon app. From a tracking chip on her shoe, her data would be uploaded to the app, and we'd see her progress mile by mile, all the way to the finish. We decided that when she passed Heartbreak Hill in Newton, still six miles and about an hour away, we'd leave the game with plenty of time to walk from Fenway Park to Copley Square and meet our other friends so that we could all watch the finish together.

......

Sabrina and I got to Fenway Park around 10:45 a.m., bought hot dogs in gluten-free buns and gluten-free beer (I have celiac disease, and Fenway has a gluten-free menu—how awesome is that?), and found our seats. The game was slow-moving, so when we got our app alert that Jen was closing in on the city, we were only into the seventh inning. But we were not going to miss seeing Jen run by us on Boylston Street, so Sabrina and I gathered our bags and headed out of the park.

We had about an hour to get through the teeming spectators and maze of closed-off streets and fight our way to our favorite spot for spectating, Forum restaurant. The drinks and food were only so-so, but the vantage point was perfect for watching runners come around the corner from Hereford Street onto Boylston and down the last half mile to the finish near the historic Boston Public Library in Copley Square.

For many spectators, and particularly those of us with friends who would take between four and five hours to finish the race, the afternoon was a long one, but if you weren't running in the marathon, cheering on a friend who was running was the second-best way to celebrate the day.

We had two friends running that day: Jen, a nurse at Mass General, and Johnny, whom I have known since the second grade. We estimated they would be finishing the marathon in about four and a half hours, or between 2:30 and 3:00 p.m. By that time in the day, over 17,000 of the 23,000 runners who began the race have already crossed the finish line, with nearly 6,000 still on the course behind them.

Sabrina and I jostled our way through the crowds in Kenmore Square and finally made it to Forum. We did a quick 360 view of the place to see if any of our friends were there yet, and, finding that they weren't, went to the bar and ordered a drink. We had no sooner arrived than we got a text from our friend Megan saying she was outside and staying there, unwilling to spend the $40 cover charge for a drink. Can't say I blamed her. Forum was hosting a fund-raising party that year, so the cover was more expensive than usual. Because the bar wouldn't let you take drinks outside, we took a quick sip of our cocktails before leaving them at the hostess station and making our way out to the sidewalk. The energy of the crowd was palpable. Once again I felt that stir of excitement in my stomach. As we got near the police barricades, I turned to Sabrina.

"Next year. Let's do it. Let's run this thing."

She looked at me, her eyes hidden behind aviator Ray-Bans but her dark eyebrows arched high above the sunglasses. She knew what would be ahead in terms of training: a training schedule that would begin in the teeth of winter, months of early-morning and late-evening runs, running clinics, even (God forbid) a drastic change in diet to skim off a few pounds. While most Boston Marathon runners have to run another marathon within a set time limit in order to qualify to run the race legally, there were plenty of charity teams you could join, so we could avoid the pesky qualifying requirement while raising money for a good cause. She could see that I was serious. Sabrina smiled and nodded.

"Okay, I'm in."

Looking around at the crowd, we finally spotted Megan and were making our way to her when a friend back at Kenmore Square texted to say that Jen had just run by him.

"She's on her way! Looks great!"

It was 2:40 p.m. Jen was just a mile away and would be arriving in less than ten minutes, maybe sooner with the adrenaline and thrill of the last mile coursing through her tired legs and pushing her forward. If you ask anyone who's ever run Boston what running that last mile feels like, most will answer in one word: "Exhilarating." The crowds thicken exponentially the closer you get, and by the time you round the last corner onto Boylston, their roar becomes deafening, forming a solid wall of energy. It's as if the joy of the crowd is channeled into the aching joints and blistered feet and screaming leg muscles of every runner.

With Megan now in tow, we all agreed that we had to get closer to the street in order to see Jen run by, so we employed some serious city-trained, sharp-elbowed positioning and got to the curb. Unfortunately, as I looked up the street to where Jen would be coming from, I realized that there was a green storage mailbox in my way. I craned my neck and stood on my tiptoes, trying to see over it. (Yes, I am that short.) But no matter how far I stretched and maneuvered, the damn thing still blocked my view up Boylston Street. While my taller friends were fine with our position, I knew I had to move. I told Sabrina and Megan that I was "going in." I shimmied through the tightly packed bodies and was able to sneak around the mailbox to its other side and squeeze myself right up against the steel police barricade. This was the perfect spot! I finally had a clear view of the runners coming down Boylston, I relaxed and settled in to watch the excitement.

Sabrina and Megan followed as far as they could but both got stopped by the crowds and ended up against the barricade on the far side of the mailbox.

At 2:47 p.m. our friends Jenna and Alissa finally made it to Forum and found us gathered near the mailbox. Unable to get anywhere near me on the opposite side of the mailbox, they squeezed in next to Sabrina and Megan along the fence.

Seeing that they had arrived, I waved to Jenna and Alissa over the mailbox, then turned back toward the race, its runners, and the sun, leaned my elbows on the barricade, and took a long, relaxed breath. This, right here, was what it was all about—standing in the midst of the fun and frenzy of Boston's best afternoon, absorbing the sheer magic of the day.

I checked my phone, as I had been doing obsessively all afternoon, for alerts on Jen and Johnny's progress.

Behind me, people gathered on Forum's patio were cheering and ringing cowbells and joking with their buddies, beers in hand, their plates of appetizers forgotten on nearby tables.

I craned my neck looking for Jen—she should be *right here*.

Jen Anstead was running her third Boston Marathon in as many years, and as in the years before had trained long and hard for this day, taking time from her demanding job as a cardiac nurse at Massachusetts General Hospital to run on the hospital's fund-raising team for pediatric cancer. Before getting into marathon running, she would have called herself merely a social runner like me, more often running the races for the after party than setting any land speed records. In fact, she was a regular at our monthly summer Thursday "Let's Run and Have Fun 5K" along the Charles River.

But a marathon was far from a fun 5K, nearly ten times as far, and Jen took her training seriously. She loved that she was now wearing a T-shirt designating her a "Team MGH" runner. She was running to raise money for pediatric oncology at Mass General helping those without deep pockets and comprehensive health insurance policies.

After four hours and eleven minutes of running, Jen finally turned the last corner of the race and onto Boylston, still not quite in my sight line. She felt an almost electric current of energy surge through her body. It seemed as if the crowd was ready to burst around her.

"YOU'RE ALMOST THERE!"

"GO, MASS GENERAL!"

"THERE'S THE FINISH! YOU MADE IT!"

Tears sprang to her eyes. Her emotions were a combination of a beta-endorphin high and the sheer joy of having the finish in sight. It was the same relief, almost a sacred deliverance, that many endurance athletes feel when finishing a multihour race. She was almost *there*. But first she had to find us and, knowing we were at Forum, trotted toward the curb in front of it.

I was standing less than seventy yards away, leaning over the steel fence, feeling it press into my armpits, trying to get my first glimpse of her. If I had had any more height or weight, I probably would have toppled the whole thing over, I was leaning so far.

Suddenly the air was shattered by an explosion. Something had blown up down the street to my left, closer to the finish line. The moment, caught on a security camera positioned above Forum's patio behind me, recorded our collective flinch as the crowd around me all reflexively hunched our shoulders at the exact same moment.

About two hundred feet from where I stood by the mailbox, Jen stopped dead in her tracks. Four police officers, patrolling the barricade, all looked over their shoulders as the blast ricocheted through the buildings and then at each other with a collective expression of "What the hell was that?" While other spectators and runners were thinking it might be a celebratory cannon of sorts, Jen knew in that instant that if the cops weren't aware of it, something terrible had happened. With people still running around her toward the finish, she stood stock still, trying to collect her thoughts and the growing realization: *Oh, my God, that was a bomb!*

······

"We need to get the *fuck* out of here."

It was Alissa, from behind me. Like Jen, her instant reaction was panic: *That was a fucking bomb.* No question. No debate.

I stood up on the barricade to see if I could see down Boylston toward whatever had exploded.

Sabrina, meanwhile, standing on the bottom rung of the barricade and leaning comfortably against the mailbox, wasn't budging. While Alissa and Jen instinctively knew the shit had hit the fan, Sabrina thought the blast was benign—a car backfiring or maybe a transformer—and she wasn't about to give up her prime spot. Sabrina watched others around her begin to move, from what and to where no one really seemed to know. Alissa's increasingly frenzied mantra of getting the *fuck* out of here felt melodramatic to Sabrina, and she all but said something. Instead she stepped down from the barricade and turned to try to reassure Alissa that whatever it was, it was nothing to worry about.

She never got the chance.

Around me people started to scatter in all directions, no one knowing what it was but everyone wanting to get away. A man near me yelled, "Jump the fence! Get in the middle of the street!" correctly guessing that whatever had caused the blast, it hadn't been sitting in the middle of Boylston Street. I looked down at the barricade I was standing on but realized I would never be able to climb over it. Even standing on it, it came right up to my chest. There was no way I could jump it. If I tried, I might hurt myself falling over the other side. I could even sprain an ankle or maybe my wrist. So I stepped off the barricade and turned to my right to run up the sidewalk.

As I was skirting a tree, I heard two loud popping sounds and saw two white flashes of light at my feet.

It was the last time I saw my right foot.

•••••

When the second bomb exploded, Jen was so close that she felt a surge of hot air rushing toward and around her. Instantly and without a word, the four cops in front of her clasped their wrists together, forming a human chain, and corralled incoming runners off Boylston and toward the Lord & Taylor store on the other side of the street, Jen among them. As she felt herself being half pushed, half carried across Boylston, a fire truck appeared out of nowhere, passing so close that the steel bumper brushed her leg and she marveled that it hadn't crushed her.

Sabrina had been blown off her feet and landed on her back a few feet away from the mailbox. Alissa, Jenna, and Megan had all turned to run but were also blown through the air, landing violently on their heads and backs among the other spectators on the sidewalk.

Anyone who had thought in the twelve seconds after the first blast that it was just a manhole cover, or perhaps a celebratory cannon, or even a ruptured gas main, knew now that both were bombs and that Boston was under attack. Those who weren't mortally wounded began running in every direction, not knowing if there would be a third bomb and, if there was, where it would blow.

Before the smoke cleared, video of the blasts shows an incredible scene: two distinct waves of people moving in different directions—the majority away from the obvious locations of the explosions and lesser numbers, many of them wearing the neon-yellow vests of police, firefighters, and medical personnel, running directly into the smoke and fire. Everywhere people were lying in ever-widening pools of their own blood. And I was one of them.

chapter two

BEFORE

IF YOU WERE to ask my mom or dad to describe the kind of kid I was, they'd immediately say the same thing: determined and stubborn as hell. Not only did I start walking when I was nine months old, I also started talking (as I write this I can hear Mom finishing the sentence, "and you haven't stopped yet.") Mom also insists I potty-trained myself. "You were *determined* never to wet your pants," she says today. "I did handstands and cartwheels trying to train your sister, Gia, and meanwhile you were telling us to stop the car or pulling on my hand to take you to the nearest toilet when you were barely a year old." Firmly resolved. She also loves to tell the story of when I was no more than two or three and my grandparents left me napping in the backseat of a car after a drive to their nephew's lake house in Merrimack, New Hampshire. At some point I woke up, found myself alone in the car, and, unwilling to wait for someone to come get me, crawled out of the open window, shimmied down the side of the car, and wandered down the road trying to find the party.

It took them many frantic, screaming moments searching the beach and the woods before they found me sitting on a nearby house's porch with a woman who evidently looked like, but was very much not, my grandmother.

It's not as if I was a bad kid—I just had too much energy and stubborn determination for my mother's taste. She had envisioned having two daughters close in age so she could dress them in matching outfits and curl their hair and prop them up on the sofa for pictures. She got her first wish, but unfortunately for her, neither Gia nor I ended up a poster girl for the well-behaved daughter nor had any interest in wearing matching Sunday-school dresses.

Our stubborn individualism wasn't her only reason for being stressed out. The other she could sum up in two words: "Your father." Ours was not *Little House on the Prairie*, particularly in the latter years before their divorce. Although Gia and I have some great childhood memories, when it was just the four of us at home in Dracut, Rose Buckley and Gene Sdoia's increasing unhappiness with each other made life anything but tranquil.

While Mom is half Irish and half Italian (maybe *that's* where I got some of my stubbornness), Dad is *all* Italian. But he's less the menacing Godfather type and more the low-key Tony Bennett type. Even with only one of them yelling (I'm sure I don't have to tell you which one), some of their fights were epic. One winter evening around dinnertime, Gia and I returned home from playing outside, back in the days when you could roam the neighborhood until it got dark. We were met on the front porch by Mom, who told us to stay outside while she and Dad "talked." As the sun set over the neighboring roofs and the evening chill set in, Gia and I huddled next to each other, trying to keep warm and waiting for the coast to clear. When we were finally allowed into the house, you could cut the tension with a knife and we could see bits of food stuck to the 1970s wood paneling in our kitchen.

······

Years later, when he'd finally had enough of the shouting and the tension and the drama, instead of telling Mom he wanted out, Dad went for a "divorce consultation" and inadvertently left the lawyer's business card on the bedroom dresser. Mom found it, and in a scene straight out of *The Sopranos*, she marched upstairs and flung the entire contents of his bureau out of their bedroom window onto the lawn and bushes below. I'm surprised she didn't set the pile on fire with the charcoal lighter fluid. My father watched the shower of his white underwear and T-shirts litter the bushes, but when she began throwing the contents of his desk over the stair railing into the family room beneath, he picked up the phone and called the police. Hearing the call, Mom finally calmed down, reapplied her makeup, put on a pot of coffee, and waited for the police to arrive.

Thirty years later, neither Mom nor Dad has remarried, although both have been with their respective partners since the divorce.

"Why would I get married again? Once was clearly enough," Mom says today.

Her opinion of having children is just about as romantic.

"It's not that I don't love you and Gia, but my advice to young women today is 'Just get a dog.'"

It won't be surprising, then, to imagine that Mom landed on the tough-love side of the parenting fence. Whenever Gia or I would come in crying with a scraped knee or a stubbed toe, her response would be a pinch on the arm or leg to distract us from the original pain with the admonishment, "Don't cry! Crying only makes you look ugly and gives you puffy eyes and a headache." Her hugging wasn't much better and usually consisted of a hand on one shoulder with an ever-so-slight lean in. Kisses on the cheek? Never in my life.

Dad was the disciplinarian and believed in the value of hard work. He always kept us busy with chores—shoveling our large driveway, stacking the firewood he'd split for the woodstove, mowing the lawn, and of course raking leaves. You name the season, and Dad had a list of chores. "It's building your character," he'd say whenever we whined about having to do more tasks before going out to play. Looking back, I realize he was trying to teach us how to be independent as we became adults, hoping we would learn how to handle life's challenges.

••••••

Gia is fourteen months older than I am. Growing up, we usually shared a bedroom, sometimes even a bed, and not always peacefully. In the bed-sharing phase, Gia's favorite game was "Steamroller," where, without warning, she would come rolling toward me and send me flying off the edge of the bed onto the floor. There wasn't a lot of peace in sharing a room, either. Where I love order—clothes in the closet and my bed made every morning—Gia is unapologetically messy and never met a hanger or a bureau drawer she liked. We remind ourselves of Felix and Oscar from *The Odd Couple*.

We also couldn't have been more different in our love lives. Where Gia married her husband, Patrick, a few years out of college and to this day is a happy wife, mom, and elementary school teacher, I was on Match.com for five years and had a grand total of six (mostly bad) dates.

March 29, 1975—My sister Gia and me at my 7th birthday party at our house in Lowell, MA.

Gia loves to tell people I'm a germophobe (true, but a slight exaggeration) and a wimp about pain and blood (used to be, although I still need to take a Valium for any serious doctor's appointment). When we were little, probably five or six, I pleaded with Mom to get my ears pierced. She immediately said no, I was too young. But after weeks of my incessant whining, Mom got sick and tired of it and finally took us both to the ear-piercing store. As soon as we entered the place and I saw its sterile, clinical environment, an animal instinct kicked in and I shook my head, insisting that Gia go first. Minutes later, when she emerged with a shiny pair of gold studs in her ears, I realized that in order to have pretty earrings hanging *from* your ears, the earrings had to actually go *through* your ears. Now that it was my turn, I immediately dug my heels into the proverbial dirt, so Mom had to drag me into the room and hold me in the chair.

23

When I heard the *pop* of the ear-piercing gun against my head and felt the stabbing pain of the stud puncturing my earlobe, it was all over. I went ballistic, and my screams brought office workers running. I left with one pierced ear and puffy eyes and a headache from the crying. (Again, Mom was right.)

Years later, I had to have a tooth pulled, and when I realized an IV was involved, I screamed and insisted that Gia be allowed in with me. Before she could even be summoned from the waiting room, I passed out. When I came to, I had a cold compress on my forehead and an oxygen mask on my face.

Just as puberty was hitting, I started to get migraines. It would take years before I was properly diagnosed with celiac disease and taken off all gluten, which finally cured the headaches. But beyond the diagnosis, it was the stifling inactivity and fear that I was missing out on something that finally cured me of my headaches, and I was back out the door as soon as I could see straight, sometimes before. I didn't care. I just didn't want to miss out on any fun.

Speaking of fun, the older I got, the more it took precedence over everything else, particularly my academic studies. I had way too much fun with my girlfriends and struggled to maintain a B average. Truth be told, if they had examined kids back then for any of the alphabet soup of "disorders," I was probably a candidate for several of them, not the least of which was ADHD.

Midway through my seventh grade and Gia's eighth grade year in junior high, Gia decided the Dracut public school system wasn't giving her enough academically and exhaustively researched available private schools before selecting Notre Dame Academy (NDA) in nearby Tyngsboro. They dragged me along to look at the school, and as we were leaving, Sister Agnes Christina gave me a hug, exclaiming, "We'll see you next year, Roseann!"

"Whoa," I said, backing away from her big arms and clutching hands. "*Gia*. You'll see *Gia*, not me."

Nope. Wrong again. Mom and Dad had signed *both* of us up. Perhaps it was missing my friends from public school or finding myself thrown into a clique of girls who had been together since kindergarten, but I never warmed to NDA. Sure, I found some friends, and I had Gia, of course, but I always felt like an outcast from the popular group of girls. It didn't help that they all carried Etienne Aigner or monogrammed Bermuda purses and wore Aigner or Sperry Topsider shoes while I carried a backpack and wore off-brand loafers. We had uniforms, thank God, because Gia and I could never even have tried to compete at the clothes level. Even so, the dress code allowed us to buy our own shirts to wear with our navy-blue skirts and matching vests. Most girls had crisp Izod polos and Ralph Lauren oxfords. Gia and I had blouses from the sale bin at Marshall's discount department store. I never fit in, or at least I felt that I didn't, and I hated that feeling. I had always had a lot of friends, and to suddenly find myself on the outside looking in was torture. So I guess it's not surprising that I would find any excuse to escape back to Dracut High School and hang out in the cafeteria, playing cards with my old buddies. It's no wonder I didn't exactly excel academically.

But it was for the summers that Gia and I both lived, spending most of the time with our grandparents, Gramma Rose and Grandpa Bill, in their rented one-room garage in Hampton Beach, New Hampshire. Every day Gramma Rose would pull a $10 bill out of her cracked leather purse and say to me and Gia and our assorted cousins, "Go buy yourselves some ice cream." We'd faintly protest that ice cream didn't cost $10, then run out the door with our booty. Every night we'd apply aloe gel to our

sunburns and brush the sand from our feet before tucking ourselves into bunk beds, day cots, pullout couches, and even a
few beach lounge chairs covered with towels. In their corner on
the pullout couch, Gramma Rose would tuck a transistor radio
under her pillow and listen to WBZ Radio's Larry Glick all night
while Grandpa Bill filled the tiny house with his throaty snores.

It was heaven.

••••••

Gia and I worked from the time we turned ten, so we always
had money in our pockets. Being older, she was first to get her
license and a car—an old beater gifted from Gramma Rose and
Grandpa Bill that leaked when it rained and had linoleum glued
to the side in an effort to retard rusting. Gia would park the
eyesore at the farthest end of the Notre Dame parking lot, away
from the other NDA girls' BMWs and Saabs and Volvos. Even
so, Gia's 1970 Chevy Impala was hard to miss.

In June of 1986 I graduated from Notre Dame Academy
and planned to follow Gia to the University of Massachusetts
in Lowell, but as a day student. A year later, when I began my
sophomore year, I convinced her to pledge the Alpha Omega
sorority with me, hoping that being a "sister" would involve us
in more and better campus activities. It did. Not only were the
sorority girls friendlier than others I had met, they were also
a lot more fun. My swinging social life was helped by the fact
that credit-card companies had just begun to realize the bounty
of easy, high-spending co-ed prey who didn't have a clue that
plastic money eventually became real debt, and the companies
trolled the student union, handing out their shiny plastic like
candy. Before I knew it, I had racked up a couple of thousand
dollars in debt on ten different cards—all of which were maxed

out. Even though I worked two jobs, and had always worked two jobs, I spent more than I earned. I knew this could be the beginning of a life of bad credit and was terrified about what that might mean for my future. It took a lot of work and a generous loan from a friend to clear the debt. I learned my lesson: to this day my only debt is mortgage.

•••••••

Throughout my four years at Notre Dame, I had had a crush on a boy back home whom I finally started dating when I got to college. He was two years older so headed off to college before I did, and when he started his senior year, I assured him that I wanted him to have a good time during his last year in college. I am not a jealous person, and I figured he could have his freedom and an unfettered senior year; then, when I graduated from college, we'd move in together, get married, and live happily ever after. I am more of a planner than a dreamer, so I was fine with him sowing some wild oats *before* we got married. But those dreams and plans disappeared in an instant. He told me he had gotten a girl pregnant and that she was moving to Dracut to have the baby. I didn't mean he should have *that* good a time!

In June 1990 my friend Sophia, who had just moved to California, invited me to come out and "have a look" at the Golden State. I did, and one morning, standing in her brother's house, brushing my teeth and looking out the bathroom window at the bluest sky I'd ever seen and a palm tree gently swaying in the ocean breeze, I realized I was in love with this place and decided I too would move out after graduation and become a California girl. And so, the following June, I packed for the West Coast with $600 in my pocket, armed with my degree in business and my sunglasses firmly planted on my head. Gia drove to California with me to help me get settled. The Chevy Impala had long since died, so we took what I called my Lego Car, a Dodge Shadow so cheap and lightweight that one day the bumper fell off in the street, and I was able to just snap it right back into place.

Just like the song, I loved LA—the warmth and the beach and the endless sun and the year-round top-down driving. I found a job as a receptionist at a realty company and then moved into the accounting department. But as much as Southern California agreed with me and I loved the friends I'd made there, I soon found that whenever I had a break from work, instead of going on exotic vacations to Europe or the Bahamas or even Hawaii, I found myself drawn back home to Dracut. I missed my family and my friends and my beloved city. And so, after two years of living and working first in California and then for a short stint in sunny Florida, I finally returned to Massachusetts for good—home, where I belonged.

After I moved back, I continued my real estate career. My company opened a division of its short-term corporate housing in Boston, and I took the opportunity to help with that project. I loved my work and moved quickly and efficiently up the management ladder. Over the next twenty-some years, I worked for three different firms in a variety of positions, working my way up to vice president of property management at National Development, a corporate, commercial, and residential real estate firm in Newton, outside Boston. I worked hard, but it was made easy because I worked with such a great group of people. And of course, there were always my weekends and summers and vacations with my friends.

But as many friends as I had, I rarely had a boyfriend. I dated, but no one stuck. Some dates failed simply because it was immediately apparent that we were not destined for the altar. Some failed for other reasons, like the time my date went on and on about how he was close to making his first million but then insisted that we go Dutch on the bill. Or the guy whose mother was still doing his laundry. Or the guy who started flirting with a different woman at the bar before our drinks were even served. Needless to say, for me the Boston dating scene was dire. And it didn't help that I often felt like the plain Jane amid my taller, thinner, blonder girlfriends and that I was always considered "one of the guys" among my male friends. By the time my forties rolled around, I was single and had settled happily into that life. Sure, I wanted to be married, but after my serious college boyfriend got that other girl pregnant, I was less than eager to jump onto any train coming through the station, and I sure as hell wasn't going to settle for some mama's boy who didn't have the manners to buy a girl a drink on a first date. I was perfectly comfortable being single until the right person came along.

I am lucky to have a city full of wonderful friends, and I love to make plans. I almost never say no when invited to join a cause, volunteer for an event, grab a beer, meet for dinner, drive to the Cape, even hop on a plane to Europe—I'm your partner in crime. Some call it a bad case of FOMO: fear of missing out. Whatever. If you have a plan, I can have my bag packed within the hour.

It was, in part, my love of being with my friends and sharing our favorite day of the year that brought me to 755 Boylston Street on that day in 2013.

chapter three

THE LITTLE WHITE SOCK

DID I WEAR SOCKS TODAY?

I was on the ground, half sitting, half lying next to the green mailbox, trying to figure out what the hell had just happened. As the smoke cleared, the first thing my mind and eyes registered was a foot in a white ankle sock—totally detached from its leg. Honestly, for a crazy minute I thought it was a movie prop, it was that cleanly severed, pristine almost.

Come on, Roseann, think. Was I wearing socks? Is that my foot?

Finally, as if trying to remember whether I'd had eggs or yogurt for breakfast, it came to me: *No, I wore flats. That's not my foot.*

A weird sort of detached relief flooded through me—I almost said, "Phew!" Then I looked down at my left leg, stretched out at an odd angle, my foot very much still attached. There was a burning tree branch on my pant leg, and, not stopping to think about my hand, I reached down and threw it off to the side. But

31

my right foot. Where was my right foot? Most of the leg was bent underneath me, but it didn't feel the way it should, kind of like when you sit on your shins. Something felt wrong. Something was missing. I could see my thigh and knee and blood that was beginning to puddle underneath the knee and pour over the curb onto Boylston Street. *Holy Mother of God, where is the rest of my right leg?*

And in that instant I knew what wouldn't be confirmed for hours: *My right leg is gone.*

Both of my eardrums had been blown out, so I felt as if I were inside a clear plastic bubble, the screams and sirens all around me a muted thudding rather than distinct, sharp noises. Where had everybody gone? The street was eerily empty except for one lone person who stood in the middle of Boylston, staring into the distance without focus. I couldn't tell if it was a man or a woman, they were so covered in soot, and their hair was straight up on their head, their clothes all but blown from their body.

I tried to make sense of why I was on the ground, deaf, burned, and with blood pouring out of my knee. Why had someone thrown a grenade at my feet? Had I done something wrong? Why would anyone want to blow me up? In what was probably seconds but felt like hours, my mind reached out for answers, but my brain was thick with confusion, moving so slowly I felt as if I was pulling it through mud to answer the most basic question: *What just happened?*

Then suddenly people were running in all directions, but none of them stopped to help me. Maybe I *had* done something wrong.

I tried to push myself up but couldn't. I felt stuck to the pavement, my legs immovable underneath me. Again I looked around as more and more people ran toward me, but none *to* me.

Little did I know that inches behind me, people lay dead and dying. Scores of others within a stone's throw had shrapnel embedded in their legs and arms and had their eardrums blown out, while others were even being burned alive by the bomb's gunpowder. I knew none of it. I thought I was all alone, rapidly bleeding to death as everybody ran for their lives. I didn't know it then, but because I was sitting up and obviously alive, the emergency responders assumed I was okay and instead focused on the two fatally wounded people behind me on the sidewalk—an eight-year-old boy and a young woman. Panic started to fill my chest, and I realized no one else could see what I could—the blood in an ever-widening puddle under my leg. While they attended to others, I was bleeding to death right before my eyes.

I looked down again, watching the blood soak the knee of my pants. With the speed of light, my mind raced, trying to find reason, answers, solutions, but all that came were a silent screaming jumble of words: *I'm going to lose my leg! I don't want to live as an amputee. I don't. I can't. But I'm still alive. I can't give up. What about my nieces and grandmother, Mom, Dad, Gia . . . I can't put them through it. Not while I have a chance to live.*

It was in that moment that I made the decision to live—and yes, if I had to, without a right leg. I didn't know how, but I would. Reaching up as much as I could, I cried out to people rushing by me, "Will somebody please help me?" It felt like the nightmare in which you scream and no sound comes out. Still, I yelled, hoping someone would hear me. "Please! Somebody help me?"

In the crazy jumble of thoughts that stumbled through my brain, one came ringing through loud and clear: *Whatever you do, Roseann, don't cry. It won't help this situation. Hold it together. And besides, it will only make you ugly.*

Gotta love Mom. She was right: I needed to focus, not cry.

Suddenly a young man, a kid, really, appeared in front of me, reaching down to pull me off the sidewalk.

Then, it hit me. *The pain.* I had been distracted by the shock of finding myself on my butt on the sidewalk, deaf and bleeding, but now the pain finally registered like a solid wall. But I didn't have time to focus on it: this kid was pulling me up off the sidewalk.

As soon as I moved, I saw that I had been sitting in a pool of my own blood. I suddenly remembered the severed foot and realized, *Oh, shit, this might be bigger, much bigger than my ruined leg.* And with that, I shut my eyes and told myself: *Do not open them until you get to a hospital. Do not.*

I know myself. And I knew without a question that if I were to look around me on Boylston Street and see other body parts and blood and death, I would lose it. And I mean lose it. Out of my mind, out of control, ballistic lose it. I am not what you'd call a brave soldier on the battlefield. So I kept my eyes shut tight.

The young guy put his arms under my armpits, and I put my arms around his neck, and he half carried, half dragged me from my sitting position on the sidewalk. We shuffled like macabre dance partners into the street. Having made the conscious effort not to look down at my right leg, I saved myself from seeing, through my shredded jeans, the exposed bones of my lower right leg, the shattered tibia and fibula like two broken broom handles, sticking out of my knee where my calf used to be, and my foot attached only by remaining pieces of muscle and skin.

As we stumbled away from the curb, crazily my thoughts again went to my footwear. *Did I wear strappy sandals today?* With a sick sinking feeling, I again remembered, *No, I wore flats.*

What was flapping around was my right foot. The thought made me so queasy, I worried I would either pass out or throw up.

"Please," I begged, "put me down. Just put me down."

Just then someone nearby said, "Put her down here, man. Gently."

They laid me in the middle of Boylston Street, my lower right leg bending beneath me at a stomach-wrenching angle, and began fumbling with my leg. I put my hands to my head, holding my eyes shut and focusing on breathing.

"This jacket's not going to work. She needs a better tourniquet," a voice said.

That didn't sound good.

"Here," a voice offered, and I felt hands move my leg as a belt was tied around my thigh.

I rubbed my head and kept my eyes shut tight against the pain and was thankful that these voices around me seemed to be handling the situation.

Suddenly another voice, I guessed a cop, given the assertive tone, told everybody, "Clear out! If you're not medical personnel, get out of here."

"You got this?" one of the voices asked.

"Am I holding it tight enough?" Even I could hear the urgency in his voice.

"No, you need to pull tighter. Good luck, man," someone said before his voiced faded into the din.

Immediately I felt hands push against my leg as the belt was pulled tight. The pain shot through my leg as if it had been hit by a baseball bat. But at least I could still feel pain. I was still alive.

The other voice spoke to me, low and steady. "I'm a physician. You're gonna be okay."

......

Dr. Collin Stultz had had a rough morning. In the midst of a nasty divorce, his mind wasn't focusing on the task at hand—revising an article on his cardiac research that was due in a couple of months to a scientific journal. After trying for a while to battle a bad case of writer's block, he decided to go down to his favorite cigar bar for a cigar and some tea. He packed up his computer and, knowing traffic would be a nightmare because of the race, put on his headphones and walked from his office at MIT across the Mass Ave Bridge to Cigar Masters on Boylston Street, a few doors down from Forum restaurant. He'd been there about an hour when he felt, rather than heard, a dull thump from out on the street. He thought little of it until twelve seconds later, when the much louder second bomb exploded less than fifty yards from the front door. Again, not even imagining it was a bomb, he was idly mulling over what the sound could be when people from the street starting pouring into the bar, screaming that something had blown up outside. Packing up his computer, he left the bar to see if he could help.

"It was a war zone," he told me later, his voice dropping a level and, even though years had passed, still registering the shock of what he had seen. "I've never been in battle, but this, this was war. Blood was everywhere. I turned to my right and walked a few feet. I saw many injured people on the ground, but they were all being cared for by emergency workers. I turned back down Boylston and then started across the street. That's when I saw you on the ground. You, by far, were the most gravely injured person I could see."

As he approached, he saw a young man holding a belt on my nearly severed leg. Assuming the young man was, like himself, an off-duty doctor or EMT, Stultz didn't question whether he, a board-certified internist and cardiologist, should take control of the tourniquet. Not only can tourniquet exchange be tricky but the young man, while nervous, looked fully in control and, as he told me, "was doing a hell of a job." Stultz checked to make sure my bleeding had stopped, and when he saw that it had, at least for the moment, he reached for my hand.

"Hold on. We're going to get you to a hospital," he said, looking around, wondering in fact when an ambulance would get there.

I squeezed his hand as hard as I could. I think the only reason I didn't break his fingers was that I had already lost a fair amount of blood and didn't have the strength.

"Come on! Get out! We're clearing the area of everyone but medical personnel."

Again, the cop, I guessed.

"Don't leave me," I said, gripping the doctor's hand even harder.

"I'm not going anywhere," he said, and then to the cop, "Officer, I'm a doctor."

Suddenly I heard a jumble of voices around me, and I felt strong hands place an oxygen mask on my face. Then a new voice appeared. I would later learn that his name was Ray Slater, and he was a recently retired captain of the Attleboro, Massachusetts, Fire Department.

Like almost everyone else watching the race on Boylston Street that day, while the confusion about *why* lingered, for Ray there was no doubt *what*: the blasts had been bombs. After the second bomb exploded across the street from where he stood, he ran toward the blast site, and he saw a man carrying a young girl whose left leg had been blown off below the knee.

Dear Jesus God. Prepare yourself, Ray.

After thirty-two years on the Attleboro fire department, he had seen countless casualties and fatalities, from charred bodies in house fires to mangled bodies in car accidents to dead, blue babies stricken by SIDS in their cribs. But this was different.

As he crossed Boylston, he could see severed and burning limbs and upward of a dozen wounded people on the ground, some of them with their legs already gone. Then Ray saw what he thought was a strange tableau: two civilians all by themselves in the middle of the mayhem around them, kneeling over a victim lying in the street. *Where in hell were the EMTs?* Even from where he was, he could see the blood.

Ferreting through an open first-aid kit from a nearby fire truck, Ray grabbed two abdominal wound dressings, the largest dressings made, and ran over to me.

Crouching down, he applied the pressure bandage, but blood immediately soaked through it, and he looked around for help to get another. As if from thin air, another firefighter* emerged and knelt down to apply another dressing. Surrounded now by several other firefighters, Ray joined their efforts to save my life.

I was determined not to lose consciousness. I was sure that if I passed out, I would die. That staying awake meant being able to fight and survive. I concentrated on taking long, slow breaths in and releasing them slowly, carefully, then repeating the Zen-like practice to keep myself calm. I continued to keep my eyes shut against the pain and the blood. I could feel it, sticky and wet, covering my left foot. Then another voice, this one a woman's, appeared above me.

---

*Later identified as Firefighter Michael Kennedy from Ladder 15/Engine 33 out of the Boylston Street station up the street.

I am lying on Boylston while Officer Shana Cottone, in the police hat, holds my hand and monitors the triage on my leg. Dr. Collin Stultz, who helped direct Shores in applying the tourniquet, is holding my left hand.

Courtesy of Bill Hoenk Photography

"I'm a police officer. My name is Shana. You're gonna be all right. What's your name?"

Even without opening my eyes, I could feel her face only inches above my nose.

"Roseann, my name's Roseann Sdoia."

"Are you with anyone, Roseann?"

"My girlfriends—are they okay?"

"I'm sure they are. Were you here watching your husband run?"

That one woke me up, and without thinking about it, I opened my eyes to see who had asked such a stupid question.

"What the hell does that have to do with anything?" I snapped. Somehow, through all the chaos and pain, it just pissed me off that the assumption was that I was there to watch a husband or a boyfriend. I went back to concentrating on my breathing. I was done with her questions and again shut my eyes. For her part, Shana was pleased: pissed-off victims are usually the ones who survive. They have fight in them.

The sirens screamed around me, and I prayed that the next ambulance was coming for me. I needed to get off the street, and I needed morphine. *Anything, really, to kill this pain.* In the meantime, I focused on holding on to Shana's hand on my right and the doctor's on my left.

"Pull harder," I heard the cop say. "You need to pull on that belt with everything you have until your hand goes numb, and then you pull harder."

I heard all of this through a haze, remembering it in more detail later when the scene was replayed over and over to the FBI, friends, and family members—and, of course, in my own head. But when she told him to pull tighter, I heard that because I knew what was coming.

A strong hand braced against my right thigh, and suddenly pain shot through my body, from my leg right up through my molars, like a jagged, dull knife. But, without even knowing it, it was that hand braced against my thigh and applying direct pressure, in combination with the tourniquet, that took my status from "actively dying" to "critical."

Then, through the pain, I heard my name being screamed.

"Oh, my God, Roseann! It's Roseann!"

I didn't have to open my eyes to recognize the voice. It was Alissa, who had stayed on the far side of the mailbox when I had sneaked around to get a better view. As the smoke cleared, she and Jenna stumbled away from the scene, finding me almost by accident as they jumped the barricades and fled across Boylston

Street. When she saw me, Alissa thought I was dead, lying in a pool of my own blood, and she began screaming.

Really? I wanted to say to her. *Really? I've lost my damn leg, and* you're *hysterical?*

"I'm all right," I said, hoping, in all honesty, to shut her up. I really didn't need her panic on top of everything else. I shut my eyes again. Officer Cottone thought she'd lost me.

"Stay with us, Roseann!" Cottone shouted, her face inches from mine.

"I'm right here," I said, although my tone said, "Back off, lady!" I could feel her fear, and it wasn't helping. Neither was Alissa's screaming. But what I didn't know was that Alissa had seen a toddler, his hair singed to his head and his face covered in blood, being carried at arm's length by a cop from the grisly scene behind me on the sidewalk. The boy was crying in fear and pain, and the cop looked as if he too were in shock. A photo of the boy and cop, one of the many iconic pictures of the bombings, ended up on the cover of *Time* magazine a few days later. The image seared itself into Alissa's brain, replaying over and over. She, like so many others, was absolutely certain that a third bomb was about to detonate or that a sniper was going to start shooting from the rooftops. Then she saw the ruination of my leg, the blood pooling around my body, and the ashen color of my face and thought, *Oh, my God. She's going to die. Roseann's going to die.* She started screaming and couldn't seem to stop.

Finally Shana told her, "You really have to shut the fuck up."

God, I love Boston cops.

Alissa took great gasping gulps of air, trying to quell the panic in her throat.

The cop turned her attention back to me. "Is there somebody we can call?"

41

Shit. That stopped me cold. *Who, indeed?*

I was very possibly dying right then and there. Who should get the call? Who could *handle* the call? Mom? Nope. Never good in an emergency and downright horrible in a crisis, Mom was not an option. Dad? His mother and his girlfriend were both very sick, so he was already dealing with a lot of worry and anxiety. Not Dad. Thankfully, as always, there was Gia. My ICE—in case of emergency—and listed as such on my phone but also, more importantly, my constant source of support in life.

"Alissa, call my sister, Gia. Call Gia."

My phone had been blasted out of my hand, and Alissa didn't have the number. Without opening my eyes, I recited Gia's number by heart.

Alissa punched in the numbers. Her hands shook so badly that she had to do it twice before the numbers were finally entered correctly. Alissa stood up, stepped away from the huddled group, and tried to pull herself together. The absolute last thing she wanted to do was to be hysterical when relaying this horrifying news to my sister. Taking a few long, deep breaths, Alissa finally hit the send button. She heard the phone ringing. Hers was one of the rare cell-phone calls that went through in the hours after the bombing. Although there were rumors that the FBI had blocked service in the Greater Boston area out of fears that the bombs had been detonated by remote control, cell-phone calls and Internet connections failed most often because of the sheer overload.

Gia, sitting in her kindergarten classroom in Plaistow, New Hampshire, looked down at her phone but didn't recognize the number, so she let it go to her voice mail. Alissa left a message: "Gia, I'm a friend of Roseann's. We're down at the marathon. She has been hurt. She's okay, but they're taking her to the hospital and she wanted me to call you. Please give me a call back. My name is Alissa." She gave her number twice, thanked Gia, hung up, and immediately called the number again, hoping to give Gia the hideous news in person rather than in a voice message.

Gia, seeing the number come up again on her phone, figured it must be important and picked up.

"Gia? This is Alissa. I'm a friend of Roseann's. I don't know if you've heard, but there's been an explosion at the marathon, and Roseann's been hurt."

Gia tried to make sense of what she was hearing and from whom. She didn't know Alissa, but she could hear the woman's thinly veiled panic. She could also hear the peal of sirens in the background.

"Hurt? How?" Gia asked.

"I think her leg is broken. There's a tourniquet on it."

Gia's heart pounded in her chest. Stunned, she did not yet fully absorb what it meant that there was a tourniquet on my leg. She struggled to regain her bearings. *Okay*, she reasoned, *Ro is hurt, but it's okay.* She was comforted, thinking that if I was able to relay her number to Alissa, I must be all right, but as she replayed the conversation with Alissa over and over in her head, she started to focus on the word "tourniquet." She had earned her nursing degree years before and knew that if a tourniquet was involved, my leg was a hell of a lot more than just broken. Still calm, she went to the principal's office, told him she was leaving, grabbed her daughter Bridget from her classroom, got in her car, and started making calls. First she called our dad, who she knew would have the marathon on television at home.

Watching the explosions live on television, Gene Sdoia had immediately reached for his cell phone. Dad knew where I would be on Marathon Monday, where I had been every Marathon

Monday since he had introduced me and Gia to the race as young girls. He tried to tamp down his rising panic as he sent me what would end up being dozens of calls and texts.

"Where are you?" "Are you ok?" "Call me!" "Are you at the marathon?" "Please! Call me!"

They all went unanswered.

Around 3:20 p.m. his phone finally rang. But it wasn't me, it was Gia. She told him I was hurt and on my way to Mass General and that as soon as she dropped Bridget at home, she was headed into the city. Dad said he'd meet her there.

Next Gia called our mother, who was unaware of the carnage in Boston and was pulling weeds in her garden when her phone rang.

"Ma, it's Gia. Are you watching the marathon?" Gia asked, trying to keep her voice even.

"No," Mom said. "The TV's on inside, but I'm out in the garden."

"Go inside. Something happened at the marathon."

Like Dad, Mom knew Marathon Monday was my favorite day of the year and that I wouldn't miss it for the world. So whatever had happened at the marathon, she knew in an instant I was in the middle of it. Hurrying into the house, Mom stopped dead in her tracks in front of the television. She felt like she was watching a replay of 9/11.

ALERT: EXPLOSION AT THE BOSTON MARATHON

POSSIBLE BOMBS AT FINISH LINE

DOZENS INJURED IN EXPLOSION ON BOYLSTON STREET

TERRORISM IN BOSTON?

The ticker-tape-like banners running underneath the picture screamed the news.

TWO EXPLOSIONS . . . A THIRD?

Over and over they played the tape of the first bomb detonating near the finish and the older runner falling to the ground from the shock wave. And then, farther up the street, a second explosion, its red ball of fire spreading into the street.

"Oh, my God, Gia! *Bombs?* What in hell is happening down there?"

Gia steadied herself to deliver the news.

"Mom, Roseann was hurt. I got a call from one of her friends who's with her at the marathon."

"Injured how? What do you mean?" Mom is not prone to histrionics, but Gia telling her I was somewhere in the middle of an explosion brought her as close to total panic as anything in her life ever had.

"They think her leg may be broken. I don't know the details, Mom. I'm coming to pick you up. We need to get into Boston fast."

"Okay. But I need to stop at the bank first. I need to get some cash."

"No, I don't want to take that much time. We won't need cash, for God's sake."

"Yes, I will. God only knows how long we'll be down there."

Gia felt a surge of frustration at our mother's 1960s mentality regarding money. No matter what, a purse had to have cash in it. The concept of credit cards and ATMs on every corner was still foreign to her, and probably always would be.

"And some cigarettes. Whatever the hell is happening, I'm gonna need more cigarettes to deal with it."

As Mom readied herself for the drive to Boston, not knowing what she would find when she got there, she too was reassured by the fact that I had been able to give Gia's number to a friend. That meant I was still conscious and alert. And she also knew

45

that a broken leg could be fixed. At least it wasn't something more serious.

······

As my mother and sister tried to make sense of what the hell had happened to me, I was still lying in the street, listening as ambulances screamed all around me. *Thank God, they're finally coming for me, and they're going to bring that morphine with them.* But they weren't. The sirens would come closer and then fade. Over and over. They were all full of other victims.

Officer Cottone was done waiting. She disentangled her hand from mine, and I heard her yell, "Get that fucking Gator over here! We gotta get her off the street!"

A Gator? Did she really mean one of those green ATVs they used at football games? We used them on the job at my property management company to move trash to the Dumpsters, for Christ's sake! My only thought was *Oh, dear God. If I don't die right here, I will when I go flying off the back of some goddamned Gator!* Not to mention the fact that the hospital was a good two miles away.

Quickly the Gator idea faded in favor of piling me into the back of a police cruiser, but then a new debate began about whether they would be able to fit me and a backboard into the car.

Oh, my God, seriously? Why can't they figure this out? All my efforts to keep my eyes shut against the chaos of voices and blood couldn't stop that conversation from coming through crystal clear. Just as the Gator versus backboard-in-the-cruiser debate started to become some kind of horrible Three Stooges routine, I heard wheels screech to a stop nearby, blissfully close.

Boston police officer Jim Davis had been parked near Kenmore Square in his paddy wagon, monitoring the radio, when he felt as much as heard the first bomb. It was a low, guttural boom. The kind you feel throughout your body. Even a mile away, he knew it was a bomb. He knew because he'd heard that sound before.

Davis began his career in Vietnam in 1973, and he was part of the evacuation of Saigon two years later. Imposing and heavily tattooed, he looks more like an aging biker than a cop, and he doesn't mind the public's confusion as he cruises the streets of Boston looking for drunks, punks, and criminals in his paddy wagon. While political correctness has tried to change the name to "prisoner transport vehicle," Davis will have none of that PC crap. It is what it is—a paddy wagon. If some are offended, let them be offended.

On Marathon Monday, Davis and his partner were on special operations, assigned to be part of the response team in case something went wrong with the marathon or the crowd. As he recalls, the 2013 Boston Marathon was the twenty-eighth or twenty-ninth he had worked. He loses count. Like many others in uniform, he considered it a good day to be on duty, part of those Bostonians who just want to have fun on a beautiful day.

By the time the second bomb blew seconds later, Davis was already lead-footing it to Boylston Street as frantic voices crackled over the police radio: *We have multiple bodies down. Bodies down. We need help down here.*

The police patrolling the barricades at the head of Boylston Street recognized Davis and his van and moved the steel fence aside. Davis drove a couple of blocks before parking the van half on, half off the curb across from where the smoke of the second bomb still lingered. He immediately got to work. As emergency crews, police, and civilians attended to the dead and dying, he did what he could do to control the crowd and keep the gawkers at bay. Knowing that the mortally wounded needed to be transported by ambulance rather than in the back of what he admitted was a filthy metal box, Davis did his best to make sure those ambulances made it in and out of the area as quickly as was humanly possible.

He looked over at the huddle around me and assumed they were stabilizing me for transport, which would, he thought, come any second now. Then he looked toward the curb and saw a victim lying on the sidewalk near the mailbox where I had been. Davis walked over and saw that the man's right leg had been blown off, and his left leg and buttocks had suffered second- and third-degree burns. Blood was everywhere, even on the first responders trying desperately to save Marc Fucarile's life.

As bad as my injuries were, Marc's were worse.

Realizing the man had minutes, not hours, to live, Davis tried repeatedly to hail an ambulance, but he got only one to stop. It had five victims in it already. *Five.* He had no idea how long it had been since he had arrived on the scene; it could have been minutes or hours. All he knew was that Marc and I would clearly bleed out if we didn't get to a hospital—fast. *But where was a goddamn ambulance?*

As Davis stood over Marc, searching up and down the street for one, Marc looked up at him and begged, "Please don't let me die. I want to see my son."

Davis paused in telling me the story months later. It took a moment for the combat veteran and streetwise cop to compose himself. The story still choked him up, and tears interrupted his words. He coughed lightly to clear his throat and then continued, telling me that when he heard Marc plead for his life, he decided he would not allow Marc to die, not on his watch, and he ran across the street to get his paddy wagon. Davis realized that filth or no filth, metal box or no metal box, his van was going to take Marc and me, the last of the still living victims, off the damn street and to a hospital.

Davis knew he might catch some flak for not following proper police procedures, but he didn't care. It was either take us in the van or leave us to die on the street. He has no regrets for making the decision he did. None.

Neither do I, Officer Davis.

••••••

When Davis's van pulled up, everyone around me flew into action. Finally—*finally*.

"Hey, Mike! Grab the head; we gotta load and go!" someone yelled.

Hands grabbed the backboard, and I felt it jerk upward with a few nauseating teeter-tottering moves before those holding the head and foot balanced themselves. Everyone seemed to be yelling at once. "Grab the belt!" "Hold that end!" "Get the doors!" "Watch her head!"

I felt the board land on a ledge and slide into place. Bodies moved around me. More voices: "You got this?" "Let me hop out!" "Get him in here too!"

Come on, come on! I silently urged. *Close the doors! Let's get moving!*

I have never been in an ambulance, but when the police-van doors finally closed, I knew something was definitely not as it should be, and I said into the darkness, "Hey, this isn't an *ambulance.*"

Understatement of the day, Roseann. But at least I was off the damn pavement.

It was 3:08 p.m., the bombs had gone off almost twenty minutes before, and I was finally going to a hospital. I wasn't at all sure I would make it alive to Mass General, but at least I was headed in the right direction.

chapter four

"STRIKE THE BOX!"

THERE WERE MANY victims that day, hundreds, but there were as many, if not more, heroes. In the years since the blast, and particularly since the trial of one of the bombers in early 2015, stories about those heroes have appeared, pretty much nonstop, in the *Boston Globe* and other newspapers. And in most of the accounts, when the first responders and other rescuers are interviewed, their overriding reaction to all the attention is "I'm not a hero. I was just doing what I could to help those who needed it."

I first heard those words directly from one of those who saved my life, Boston firefighter Mike Materia.

Before I met Mike, my knowledge of Boston's fire history was limited to perhaps its most famous and ghastly tragedy: the Cocoanut Grove nightclub fire of 1942. I had heard about the fire many times growing up because Gramma Rose, Mom's mother, had been all set to go to the club that night with her girl-friends, but her parents had a hard and fast rule that she be ac-companied by at least one of her five brothers. For some reason, none of her brothers would go, so Gramma had to stay home. Several of her girlfriends were among the 492 people who died that night, trapped by the crush of bodies in the revolving front door and exit doors that opened inward, rather than out, burning them alive while onlookers and would-be rescuers, unable to reach them through the inferno, listened to their screams. The tragedy would be one of the major catalysts in instituting regulations mandating that exit doors open outward.

All of the nation's older cities, Boston included, have suffered their share of catastrophic fires. Boston has had at least six, the first dating back to 1711. But unlike the great fires of New York, Philadelphia, Chicago, Washington, and even New Orleans and St. Louis, Boston's many fires have killed relatively few citizens and firefighters through the years. The Cocoanut Grove was a gruesome exception.

Within the Boston Fire Department, the 1972 Hotel Vendome fire stands as the worst loss of life for firefighters and haunts the city's firehouses to this day. As firefighters were doing a routine sweep of the hotel after having contained the fire without any loss of life, a section of the building collapsed without warning, burying Ladder 15 and trapping seventeen firefighters in the rubble, killing nine.

Thirty-five years later Mike Materia joined that same Ladder Company 15 out of the Boylston Street fire station.

••••••

Mike was born on November 14, 1979, and raised in a small town thirty miles south of Boston. At the precise moment of his birth, the hospital was shaken by a fire emergency, and even though the alarm was blaring through the delivery room, the doctor ordered everybody to stay where they were so he could "get this baby delivered." So Mike entered the world amid sirens and heavy-footed firemen traipsing through the maternity ward. In addition to that foreshadowing of his future career, Mike was weaned on stories of fires and those who fight them. On his father's side of the family, his grandfather, two uncles, and one cousin were all New York City firefighters. On holidays, they would invariably be working rather than spending the day in their own homes, so Mike and his father would visit them on duty. Over the years, he heard stories of countless fires and the damage they caused, but he also learned about the many, many lives that firefighters had saved. These are the men and women who go headlong into the inferno, over and over, making sure that they haven't left anyone behind. Even at a young age, Mike recognized a simple fact about these people: they loved their job. And, unlike the relatives on his mother's side of the family, who were, in his mind, successful but gloomy businessmen, his paternal grandfather and uncles were happy working in small teams, helping people, doing good. They and their fellow firefighters were like brothers, trusting each other and working toward a common goal, and Mike wanted to be part of that kind of team one day.

Mike's dad, Col. Joseph Materia, says he was a quiet, serious boy who always wanted to do everything right while avoiding the limelight as much as possible. He also did everything he could to avoid his mother. His family told me she was a volatile woman, and Mike said he learned early to keep his mouth shut to avoid her wrath. She seemed to him unhappy being a mother and in her marriage, and she took it out on her two young children. Whatever the cause of her bitterness, Mike learned never to rely on her for help with homework or problems at school. Instead he went to his father, always the loving and available parent, sometimes having to wait until late in the evening, when his dad came home from work. Mike and his father loved to sit and watch old movies together—a John Ford classic or *The Charge of the Light Brigade* with Errol Flynn. Through the years, Mike's tendency to avoid conflict made him reluctant to express any anger. Even when provoked by kids at school, he never hit back. His teachers always said Mike was a gentle giant, but sometimes his parents worried about his unwillingness to defend himself.

Perhaps because of the tension at home, Mike became a worrier. From an early age, he fretted over homework, test results, reprimands. It didn't take much for Mike's stomach to tighten with nerves. He was also the kind of kid who was always hard on himself. What frustrated young Mike most was his own failure at something—striking out in baseball, missing a tackle in football, or a bad grade on a math test. He always took responsibility when something didn't go well, never blaming the pitcher or the referee or his teachers.

Mike's dad says that even as a kid, he always wanted to make sure that everybody he cared about was taken care of. And as Mike made his way through twelve years of Catholic school, he set two goals for his future: first to serve like his father in the military and then, like his grandfather and uncles, to serve in a fire department.

Mike found that he was a quick study to whom things came easily, history being his favorite subject. While A's came effortlessly in his other subjects, his B-average math scores disqualified him as a candidate for West Point, which his father and uncle had both attended. Instead he received a full scholarship to attend Stonehill College in Easton, Massachusetts.

Then, in September 2001, only a few days into his senior year of college, the world changed forever. The moment the planes hit the World Trade Center, Mike's desire to serve became even more personal. Mike's uncle, New York firefighter Phil Prisco, was off duty that morning, but as soon as he heard the news, he immediately headed to his firehouse. Meanwhile, men from his company jumped into their trucks and were in the tunnel between Brooklyn and Battery Park when the World Trade Center came cascading down above them. Mike's reaction to this act of terrorism, like that of many Americans, was *Never again. Never.* He had already begun his military training, but after 9/11 he knew without a doubt that he would be heading somewhere in the Middle East. While Mike's college buddies were obsessing about their work-study programs at Morgan Stanley and their internships with W. B. Mason, he felt himself already separating from that sort of civilian life and its seemingly trivial worries. He knew he was headed into a real firestorm and that he would soon be in the middle of the hot, sandy war zone.

After graduating from college in May 2002, he was commissioned as an officer, graduated near the top of his class, had further military occupational specialty training, and was soon a second lieutenant with the Third Battalion, Tenth Special Forces Group, where he worked in various roles as a support officer in Iraq and then Qatar. Even though he was relatively low on the army totem pole, his quiet competence quickly earned him the respect and even tutelage of some of his superiors.

●●●●●●

Mike's three tours of duty gave him a lot of time to think about his next steps. On the rare mornings when the desert was still cool before the sun got too high in the sky, Mike would sit at his remote outpost with a cup of hot coffee and gaze at the strange, violent world around him. *Don't even think about missing this place when you go home,* he'd warn himself. But still, the land had an ancient and untouched beauty he loved. When he had first learned where he was going to be stationed, he'd read everything he could get his hands on about Iraq—devouring the rich and troubled history of a land that Genghis Khan, Alexander the Great, the Mongols, the Turks, the Ottoman Empire, and of course the British had all tried and failed to tame. Always a processor of information, Mike tried to analyze why this land and these people forever found themselves in the crosshairs of conquering armies.

During his deployment, he and the other men in his company and, even more so, the smaller squad of soldiers saw and averted death. While he had several close calls, he nonetheless loved being part of a close-knit team, all putting that team above self, working toward a common goal. He had learned the love of group effort in high school football, but it became ingrained in the army. And with that shared adrenaline rush came something much, much deeper: a love, yes, of each other but also of the entire tribe, and defending that tribe, keeping it as safe as possible, became their goal. Living and dying for each other became the fabric of their life, and every man felt it and cherished it. And every man in that company felt its irreplaceable loss when he retired from the service.

After his third and final tour in 2007, now Captain Michael Materia knew it was time to leave before he burned out. Besides, he was ready to move back home, join a fire department, and settle into the rest of his life. Because he loved both New York and Boston, he could see himself happy in either city's department. But as fate would have it, an opportunity to take the Boston Fire Department test came first. He passed and got his name on the first of many lists in the BFD's protracted hiring process. In March of 2007, he finally set his boots back on US soil and immediately moved to the city to establish residency, another prerequisite of joining the department. Several months later, he earned a slot in the training classes, and by the fall, he was given his assignment.

To this day, Mike doesn't know how he managed to be assigned to the Boylston Street firehouse, arguably the city's most legendary and architecturally illustrious station. Built in 1888, it remains Boston's most beloved firehouse. Some of his fellow recruits even asked if Mike knew some big shot in city hall or the State House who had pulled patronage strings to get him stationed there. Mike just shrugged and told them, "Nobody. My family's from New York."

Just a few months after retiring his army uniform, Mike found himself in his dream job in one of Boston's most storied companies—Engine Company 33 and Ladder Company 15. Mike instantly loved being part of 33/15. He'd sit outside the station, sipping coffee, thinking how impossibly different his early-morning view in Iraq had been from this one on Boylston Street and realizing with happy satisfaction, *I'm home.*

As he sat, he watched people walk by on their way to work, and imagined the men who had come before him. Mike wondered what they would think of the modern heavy protective bunker gear, given that in the old days the men would run headlong into a fire with little more than a raincoat against the flames and their dampened beards to filter the smoke. Just as he had with the military, he loved being a part of a venerable institution that was defined by collective survival. No one wins wars or fights fires alone.

Maybe because he had focused so intently on school, then college, then training for the army, then deployment, then the fire department, Mike had never really devoted much time to his love life. His quiet nature, his penchant for reading, and then his years in the military and those demanding deployments had instilled in him an ability to appreciate the little things: traveling, watching 1980s movies, hanging out with a few buddies, watching a game, drinking a beer, and sharing a pizza or two. He'd had girlfriends along the way, each relationship lasting almost exactly a year—a trend his friends called his "One-Year Itch." While he was stationed overseas, the challenges of a long-distance relationship wore on him. As he sat in Iraq, looking at the ruins of war all around him, he felt impatient as he listened to complaints from a girlfriend about how she needed a new cell phone or that someone had snubbed her at the bar. He knew the complaints were real to her, but from his frontline perspective, they felt trivial and self-absorbed. For these and a host of other reasons, no romantic relationship had stuck. Not only was he distracted by life, he also did not want to make the same mistakes his parents had made, particularly after watching their troubled marriage and bitter divorce. He wanted to make damn sure he found the right one.

But I think the real reason is simply that he has never been in a hurry. He wasn't desperate to find a mate. He has always been perfectly happy lying low, keeping under the radar, and maintaining his innate balance while the rest of us seem to flail about in our crazy universe.

•••••••

On April 15, 2013, Mike arrived at the fire house for his twenty-four-hour shift a bit earlier than usual, about 5:30 a.m., in order to find parking before police shut down that area of Boston for the marathon, which would soon to be winding through its streets. He loved working on race day, unlike many of his buddies in the department who took the day off to enjoy the city's largest street party. The Boylston Street firehouse is arguably the city's most visible and most popular station, and on Marathon Monday it is a destination for spectators and tourists who are shown around the iconic building by its firefighters, all of whom are proud to call it home.

After lunch Mike stood on the brick entranceway in front of the station house, watching the crowds and soaking up the sun. Situated on the corner where the race takes a ninety-degree turn from Hereford Street onto Boylston, the Engine 33/Ladder 15 firehouse was the perfect vantage point for watching the marathon and the tens of thousands of (often tipsy) spectators milling around it. He checked his watch: 2:49. It was still early. The after party for runners and spectators alike had really just begun.

Four hundred and fifty miles to the south, Mike's father, Col. Joe Materia, sat in his office at the Pentagon, working with an ear toward his scanner, monitoring the radio traffic on the Boston Fire Department channel. It was something he did whenever Mike was on duty.

Mike calls his father a "spark," an affectionately ribbing term for a fire nerd, someone, usually a nonfirefighter, whose hobby is knowing everything and everyone involved with firefighting. That's definitely Joe Materia. This fascination began when he was a boy, watching his father and then brothers head off to their jobs on various engines and ladder trucks, and it intensified after 9/11, when his brother-in-law Phil had been one of the thousands of first responders at the rubble that had been the World Trade Center. After years of listening to the firefighting channels in various cities where his loved ones were stationed,

Joe could get as much information from the tone of the firefighters' and dispatchers' voices as from the actual words they were saying. Even in the face of utter mayhem, first responders are trained to stay calm and impartial as they relay critical information to get help where it is needed and get it there fast. There's no room for histrionics and exaggerations.

At 2:49 p.m. on Marathon Monday, Joe heard a call come over the radio on Mike's firehouse channel, and even the tone chilled his heart: "There's been an explosion on Boylston Street. STRIKE THE BOX! STRIKE THE BOX!"

Not only did Joe hear a desperate urgency in the voice of the firefighter who made the call, he also knew that when the alert involves the command to "strike the box" for anything other than a large building fire, something catastrophic has happened. The term has its origin in the mid-1800s, when Boston instituted the nation's first telegraph-based fire-alarm boxes positioned throughout the city's neighborhoods, with each box having its own number and representing a certain section of the city. Over the years, other cities' alarm boxes have been updated by more modern and quick communication systems, but in Boston, the base technology of its 3,462 box alarms remains the telegraph. In an age of cell phones and satellites, the telegraph lives on in the old red boxes on thousands of street corners.

To strike, or hit, the fire box means to call out every available emergency vehicle in the neighborhood to respond. That "box" routinely involves three to four engines, two ladder trucks, a rescue company and its large utility truck filled with various emergency tools, a fire chief, the chief's assistant, and various other fire-support companies, usually EMS units with one or more ambulances. It also usually brings the police to the scene to do any necessary crowd control and street monitoring. When

Joe heard that there'd been an explosion and that the response was to strike the box, he knew it wasn't a simple, controlled event. This was an all-hands-on-deck emergency. And Mike was in the middle of it.

Back at Mike's station, the explosion half a mile away down Boylston Street had stopped everyone in their tracks. Every head made a collective snap to the left, looking down the street for the source.

Maybe it was a manhole cover, Mike thought, *or a transformer blowing somewhere*. As one of those trained not to overreact in emergency situations, Mike struggled to make sense of what had just happened, refusing to let his imagination get the better of him.

But twelve seconds later, when the second device exploded even closer to where he stood in front of the fire station on Boylston, he knew instantly what they were: bombs.

Mike jumped up and ran toward Engine 33, which he had been assigned to that day instead of his usual perch on Ladder 15, parked fifty yards away.

"Hey, where's the fire?" a smart-ass college kid yelled from his stool at Dillon's, a nearby bar, cracking himself up along with his drunk buddies.

Mike ignored them and kept running to the engine, where he threw on his full bunker gear—three-layer coat and pants, helmet and hood, rubber boots, and thick gloves. Even without the oxygen tank, the gear weighed close to twenty-five pounds, and wearing it always felt like he had on an enormous ski suit in the summer—hot and cumbersome. Nevertheless, he piled on the gear and climbed into the engine, feeling an electric current run through him, part adrenaline, part urgency. He needed to get there. *Fast.*

Easier said done. Not only is downtown Boston effectively a gridlocked, shut-down city on Marathon Monday but all vehicles, even fire engines, are blocked from heading down Boylston Street by the same thing that blocked me from getting off the sidewalk and into the middle of the street: four-by-ten-foot heavy metal police barricades that create a solid 3.5-mile fence, lining both sides of the marathon route from Cleveland Circle in Newton all the way to the finish.

Engine 33 and Ladder 15 approached the barricade and stopped. The police standing nearby seemed oddly still, as if they were catatonic, staring at the billowing smoke down the street. No one seemed able or willing to make a decision about what the hell had just happened and what to do about it. Compounding the situation was a general hesitation by all emergency crews—police, fire, even EMS—to go against a hard-and-fast rule: *Don't ever drive onto the marathon route. Too many civilians.*

But, like all veterans who have seen their share of combat, Mike had learned another hard-and-fast rule: adapt and overcome. In other words, proper emergency responses, particularly those in combat, rarely follow textbook rules. Every soldier has to be able to think for him- or herself and move, act, and react, very likely without the command coming from above. As the engine approached the barricade, every fiber of Mike's body was screaming, GO.

"Fucking drive over it!" Mike yelled. "Mow it down! JUST MOVE!"

Behind Engine 33's wheel, Frank Lang, another combat veteran who'd done four tours in Iraq with the marines, leaned on the earsplitting air horn. In front of them, Tommy Cherry drove Ladder 15, struggling to inch it forward.

With the siren blaring and cops standing stock-still, a couple of civilians finally took action and pulled the fence aside, allowing Engine 33 and Ladder 15 to finally move down Boylston. Mike saw what looked like a bull run of people coming toward him—stunned spectators and marathon runners, most of whom were unaware of what had actually happened and were trying to decide whether they should keep heading toward the finish or turn and join the wall of spectators running away. Further adding to the confusion were scores of neon-yellow vests beginning to flood the area—police, EMTs, marathon workers—all moving toward the second bomb site and its victims.

Down at the site of the first bomb, things weren't any better, judging by the traffic Mike heard on his radio before switching it off, feeling like it was futile. There was so much traffic on the channel that it was impossible to hear any distinct call—it was all just noise. In fact, the radio was so scrambled by the many screaming voices, and the scene so chaotic, that many of the police and emergency crews at the site of the first bomb weren't even aware that there had been a second bomb two hundred yards up Boylston until some minutes later. Adding to the general chaos was the fact that in a mass-casualty event, the Emergency Medical Service is in charge of handling the scene, not the police or fire departments. When the first bomb went off, the EMS director positioned near the finish line became totally engaged in handling *that* mass-casualty event. But when the second bomb went off up the street, there was no one in charge to take control of the second site. So as the police, fire, and emergency crews rushed in to help the wounded, they had no one to organize the chaos, issue orders, and oversee the reaction. Trained to work and think in teams, they were suddenly all individuals. It was, quite literally, every police officer, firefighter, and civilian assessing the scene for him- or herself, taking any action they could.

Engine 33 drove toward the lingering smoke of the second bomb rising above the shattered storefronts of Forum and Starbucks next door, and Mike tried to organize his triage plan. But in order to devise his course of action, he needed to know the nature of the event. If it was a building fire, he knew what to do—secure his helmet, oxygen tank, heavy fire-resistant coat, and ax before hopping off, grabbing the "line," or hose, and, depending on whether they were the first or second unit on the scene, entering via the front, rear, or roof of the building. If it was a car accident with casualties, he'd don his rubber gloves, grab his green oxygen bag, which also contains emergency medical triage supplies, and stabilize the patients before handing them off to the better-equipped ambulance crew. But this time he had no idea what lay ahead of him other than some sort of explosion. And they were headed into the heart of it.

"Fuck," he muttered. "God*damn* it." Training 101: personnel don't ever enter an area until it's been secured. The life of the soldier who's been hit cannot be saved by the loss of the lives of his rescuers. Everything he'd learned about bombs or IEDs, improvised explosive devices, was that insurgents would often "daisy chain" them: first create an event with one bomb, then wait for responders to swarm into the "kill zone" and attack the real targets—anyone in uniform. And there he was, a uniformed man heading straight for the source, not knowing if there were two bombs or twenty-two.

As his mind raced for a solution, it also quieted. Years of training and maneuvers with the army and now the fire department kicked in, and Mike felt a preternatural calm about what might be coming next. Studies of the varying levels of calm in the face of danger among people in various professions have revealed that the level of danger has very little to do with a person's level of fear, but it has everything to do with their sense of control. Fighter pilots, for example, who are highly trained and entirely in control of the plane, if not their own fate, reported much lower levels of fear than their usually less-experienced turret gunners. But as well trained as Mike was to face and control danger as a soldier and a firefighter, being in the middle of a still-unfolding terrorist attack in the middle of thousands of civilians on the streets of Boston threw all of that training out the window. What remained was only his ability to adapt and overcome.

Mike took a deep breath. *Okay, let's get to work*, he thought. *If they're gonna get us, they're gonna get us, but we're going in.*

Mike jumped out of the truck, grabbed his green oxygen bag, and hurried toward a group gathered near a green mailbox. As he approached, they parted to let him through. Memories from the war in Iraq flashed through his brain—chiefly the smell of blood on hot pavement and burning human flesh. The horrors of war had prepared him for violence, bloodshed, and innocent victims, but no training in the world could have prepared him for what he saw on Boylston Street that beautiful Monday afternoon: the violence of the battlefield, but at home, where he worked, on his streets, in America. The first person he saw was a young boy lying on the sidewalk. Moments before, the boy had been standing on the barricade trying to decide what flavor ice cream he'd get when they left the marathon. But before ice cream, his family had decided to watch the race for just five more minutes.

Mike knelt next to the boy and reached for his medical bag. In the moments since he had put it down, it had already been rummaged through by other rescuers and bystanders looking for anything to stem the flow of blood for the many victims. He swallowed his rage at their arrogant pilfering of his critical supplies and then focused on the boy.

Mike took a deep breath, trying to steady himself. For years he had greeted young boys at the fire station, boys who would look up at him with wide-eyed admiration. Having been that little boy himself, he recognized the purity of the hero worship. And here he was, kneeling over a boy who could very well have been a recent visitor to the Boylston Street station, maybe even earlier that day.

He worked on the boy for what seemed like a lifetime, though it was really more like four or five minutes. All around him, people scrambled through the chaos. He was used to working in a team. Here, everyone was forced to work as an individual, grabbing supplies and running from person to person, body to body, trying to help. There were so many. Less than five feet away, he saw a police officer administering CPR to a small, dark-haired woman whose legs had been pulverized by the blast, her femoral arteries and veins almost certainly severed.

Boston police officer Lauren Woods had been on a routine shoplifting call across the street in the Prudential Center mall when she'd heard the first bomb and then the second bomb and had run out to the street. She saw the smoke lingering in front of Forum and rushed over to an opening in the cluster of bodies bent over victims. She saw a young woman lying on the sidewalk whose legs had been destroyed in the blast and around whom a puddle of blood quickly spread. While others placed belt tourniquets on what remained of the woman's legs, Woods saw that she had vomit around her mouth, turned the woman's head to the side, and used her fingers to clear it as best she could from her throat. She found the woman's ID in her purse and bent over her, urging, "Stay with us, Lingzi. You're going to be okay, but you have to stay with us."

Lingzi Lu, a graduate student from China, lay with her eyes open, staring at the sky. Woods looked at her for a terrible, quiet moment and, thinking her still alive, bent low and repeated, "Please, stay with us."

......

Nearby, Mike had moved away from the young boy and looked toward the small group gathered around Lingzi Lu. She lay still, unresponsive. Woods was desperately administering CPR. Mike knelt down, trying to determine what he could do until the EMTs arrived. He reached into his triage bag for another oropharyngeal airway and tried to insert it into her throat, but vomit still clogged the airway. He reached for a suction bulb, a slightly larger version of those used to clear ear wax, and tried to clear as much vomit as possible. But as fast as he suctioned it out, vomit again filled her mouth. Even as he struggled to get air into her body, he knew that she had lost too much blood and that there was nothing he could do to save her. He had to move on. Mike again moved away, looking for someone he could help.

Behind him, an ambulance finally approached. The EMS crew got Lu on a backboard, and Officer Woods helped them lift her in. But just before the doors closed, one of the EMTs realized the young woman was already dead. "She's gone; take her out. We need to move those who are still alive."

Lu was laid on the sidewalk where she had died.

By the time Mike saw me lying in the middle of Boylston Street, there were several firefighters and bystanders hovering over me. A college-aged kid was pulling on a leather belt applied to my right leg, my hair was singed straight up, and burns covered my right hand and arm.

It was about 3:07 p.m. when he approached my huddle, nearly twenty minutes since the explosions. *Where in the hell is an ambulance?* he thought. *Why is this woman still lying in the middle of Boylston Street?*

As he was moving toward us, I felt strong hands gently maneuver a backboard underneath me and slowly slide it the length of my body, not an easy task given the state of my lower half. Before I could register what they were doing, I felt hands take the pieces of my right leg and its shattered bones and in one swift jerk straighten it out in order to put it in a splint. Whether it had been the shock, the adrenaline, or both that had kept the pain somewhat manageable, at that moment the pain became searing agony. I felt, rather than heard, my scream reverberate through my body and down the street.

Mike saw a paddy wagon approach, and he ran over to where two of his buddies from the Ladder 15 crew, Tommy Cherry and Michael Kennedy, were struggling with the backboard. Kennedy saw him coming and yelled, "Hey, Mike! Come grab the head. We gotta load and go!"

Ray Slater, the retired Attleboro fire captain, was holding on to one of the backboard corners. He was happy to see the six-foot-one-inch giant hop into the paddy wagon and reach back out to take hold of the top of the board, pulling it and me into the truck with him. Slater climbed in with his end, helping slide it onto the bench.

The college kid, Shores Salter, still holding the tourniquet, climbed up onto the running board, unsure what to do next.

"You got this?" Shores asked Mike.

Mike, having had no time to assess the situation, evaluate the patient, or plan the triage, had no idea who this kid was—a young nurse or maybe even a doctor, or maybe the woman's brother. Either way, the kid was utterly calm, even seeming to be in command of the chaotic situation while others around him were losing their shit. Mike was impressed, but he also smelled alcohol on the kid's breath and guessed correctly that he was one of the many thousand college kids who spent Marathon Monday cruising the bars. Mike looked at the kid's bloody hands and felt a surge of empathy. Nothing had prepared this young man for this kind of mass murder, yet here he was, doing what few others had done: helping keep this mortally and grotesquely wounded woman alive. Nobody likes blood, even trained emergency workers, but this kid was up to his elbows in it.

"Yeah, I got this, thanks," Mike said, and Shores jumped out, back onto Boylston Street.

Ray Slater found himself trapped at the far end of the van, Mike's imposing figure now kneeling on the floor, blocking the narrow passageway between the benches. Seeing that they were about to load another victim, Ray reached out, as he had with my headboard, to help load a man even worse off than I was: Marc Fucarile, whose right leg had been totally severed at the thigh and whose left leg had been badly burned. Ray knew he had to move fast or he was going to get trapped in the back of the wagon and ride to the hospital with them. Climbing over Mike, he hopped out onto the sidewalk. Another firefighter, Pat Foley, who had been part of Fucarile's triage on the sidewalk, jumped in with his backboard.

When Mike and Foley loaded me and Marc into the van, both had to climb in with their "patients." Unlike their usual protocol of handing off the injured to EMTs with a fully equipped and clean ambulance, the firefighters had no choice but to accompany us because the only thing inside the paddy wagon was metal—two benches, floor, walls, and ceiling. No lights, no windows, and, most importantly, no straps to hold me and Marc and our backboards on the benches.

Officer Shana Cottone shut the steel doors and pounded on the side of the van. "Let's GO!" she yelled as she jumped into the cab with Officer Davis, who was behind the wheel.

Twenty minutes after the second bomb, the scene was finally cleared of victims: Marc and I were two of the last to be transported out.

When Officer Cottone shut the van doors, our world inside the paddy wagon went black. And it stank. Layers of criminals' filth, body fluids, and desperation filled its tight quarters. Almost choking on the stench, Mike switched on the flashlight attached to his coat and wondered if the police ever hosed out the fetid boxes. What I didn't know was that the worst of the smell came from me and Marc on the other bench: the stench of our singed hair, burned skin, sticky blood, and various other body fluids filled the airless metal box. It would take weeks for Mike to clear the stink from his body and nose.

I was still terrified, sure that losing consciousness meant losing my life, but at least I was finally moving toward the hospital, even if it wasn't in a properly equipped ambulance. Soon others would be in charge of saving my life. Now I refocused on getting morphine and how soon I would be free of this unrelenting pain.

"My name is Mike," the firefighter hovering over me said, introducing himself in his usual routine for trying to keep critically injured people calm. "We're gonna get you to the hospital as fast as we can."

Through the metal wall behind my head, I could hear someone yelling. It was muffled, but I could hear "GET THE FUCK OUT OF THE WAY!" clearly enough. Sounded like Shana, the cop from the street. The sheer power of her voice gave me comfort, and I was glad that of all the people to escort me to the hospital, I had a take-no-prisoners woman cop who was not about to let some daydreaming numskulls slow my progress to Mass General.

Finally, as the van inched off Boylston Street, the crowds thinned, and I felt the van pick up speed. Soon my backboard was sliding perilously around on the bench. Mike knelt on the putrid floor and braced his hand against the slimy wall. I felt rather than saw his torso, made even more imposing by his heavy firefighting coat, create an immovable wall, holding me securely in place on the bench.

I tried not to think about the germs marching off the foul bench and into my open wounds. Anxious and uncomfortable, I bent my left leg to try to change my position and better balance myself as the van careened through the streets. As I did, I heard rather than felt a splash of blood. The sound of my own blood splashing onto the backboard immediately made me gag, and I had a moment's fear that I would vomit, making things worse, to say nothing of further damaging my leg.

Don't you dare throw up, Roseann. Don't you dare. I clenched my jaw hard against the bile in my throat and the stench.

Mike looked down at my leg in the splint on the backboard. What he saw made his heart stop: in the mayhem of loading me into the van he had not seen the condition of my leg or that there was a tourniquet around my right thigh. It had happened in a flash of blood and confusion. Shores, untrained in emergency protocol, hadn't known to tell Mike that he was holding an improvised tourniquet, and with my leg in a splint and my pant leg covering the worst of the damage, Mike had been at my head, focusing on getting me into the van, and hadn't seen the belt.

Emergency training 101: once applied, you never, ever let go of the tourniquet because the pressure that builds up behind it will cause the blood to all but explode from the limb once it's loosened. But what they often don't teach you is that maintaining the pressure on any tourniquet becomes more and more difficult as the body fights to restore its blood pressure. When the arteries and veins in my leg were severed, my blood pressure crashed, from about 110 to 40 or 50. Almost immediately a multitude of lifesaving mechanisms kicked in to try to keep blood flowing to the organs most at risk: heart, lungs, brain, and in my case kidneys, which would later come to the brink of failing. Somewhere en route to the hospital and flying around on that bench, my blood pressure temporarily "recovered," soared substantially higher, and now my blood gushed with newfound power out of my ruined leg.

Mike tried as best he could to steady himself against the bench. He took hold of the belt, slick with blood, and pulled it with everything he had. He wished he had a CAT, or combat-applied tourniquet, used on battlefields for decades, which he could have secured in place with its self-locking device. Instead he tried desperately to tighten the slippery leather belt on my leg as the van continued to careen through the narrow streets of Boston. And just when he thought things couldn't get any worse, I reached out, found his hand where it was braced on the wall, and grabbed it.

"Please, hold my hand."

Mike did, taking his hand off the wall to do so. But, feeling the burns on my hand, which were already oozing, he tried to hold my wrist instead. His medical training had been very clear about burns and their susceptibility to infection, and he didn't want to make it any worse by introducing into my burns the filth that had been smeared all over him on Boylston Street.

But I didn't know any of that then. Even if I had, I'm not sure I would have cared.

"No," I insisted, hitting him in the chest and grabbing for his hand. "My hand. Hold my hand." Suddenly holding that firefighter's hand became survival itself, as if life was flowing through it directly into me.

Mike realized what I couldn't articulate: that holding my hand was the only thing keeping me from totally losing it. He took my hand.

As the van picked up speed, I asked Mike, "Are we on Storrow Drive? I want to go to Mass General. We should be on Storrow Drive."

With one leg blown nearly off, the other badly burned and bleeding, my eardrums blown, and my hands an oozing mess of burned skin and blisters, my Google Maps mind was nevertheless fully operational. Even through the darkness I felt as if I could see Mike's eyes roll, like an exasperated spouse at one too many questions about our route to Cape Cod that weekend.

"Relax, you're gonna be okay. We're almost there," he told me, hoping to God they were.

Suddenly a cell phone rang. I almost laughed. It felt like a very bad iPhone commercial—that in the midst of this mayhem, someone somewhere was idly calling their buddy. It came from Marc, the guy on the other bench.

"Please," I heard him say, "can you answer that? It's my girlfriend."

I heard a rustling and then another male voice.

"This is Pat Foley speaking. I'm a Boston firefighter. I'm with your boyfriend. We're on our way to the hospital. You should come as soon as you can."

I heard Marc groan, then go absolutely still. I wondered if he was dead.

"Am I going to die?" I asked Mike, squeezing his hand.

He was silent for a moment before he answered. "No, you're fine. It's only a flesh wound."

It would take me weeks to appreciate the irony, and tenderness, in that comment.

I squeezed his hand harder, adding, "Don't let go, Mike. Please, don't let go."

chapter five

BOSTON'S FINEST—
POLICE OFFICER SHANA COTTONE

"IF ANY COP tells you they weren't afraid, they're fucking lying to you," Officer Shana Cottone told me once, her voice hard and vulnerable at the same time and laced with a thick accent, part Long Island, part Boston. And during that day, "I was petrified."

She was petrified because she was absolutely sure she was going to die. Like Mike, she had learned in her training that the first attack kills randomly to draw the police, fire, federal, state, and other various emergency crews. Then a second attack is often planned to hit the real targets—usually anyone who in any way represents the government. September 11th had been an example of just such a one-two punch attack (as have more recent bombings and shootings in Mumbai, Paris, and Brussels, and closer to home in San Bernardino and Dallas).

Shana hadn't signed up for this—terrorism on the streets of Boston. If she had wanted to deal with bombs and body parts, she would have joined the military, not the Boston Police. She was not prepared to watch her own city blown apart, torn down the center, forever changed, and to know that its near-sacred marathon would never again be a day of pure fun and carefree celebration.

Shana was scared, but she was also angry—angrier than she could ever remember being, and that was saying something. Not quite a hothead, she was nonetheless known for her inability to suffer fools, on the job or on the streets. During her five years on the police force, her beats had included two of Boston's seedier neighborhoods, East Boston and Roxbury. There, she thought she had seen it all—murder, child abuse, domestic violence, knives, needles, guns, prostitutes, drugs, and gangs.

But what she saw on April 15, 2013, just plain pissed her off. How dare some faceless creeps do this to innocent men, women, and children? Especially children. During her years in the department, she had seen a lot of victims, some of whom weren't always that innocent. But the children were always innocent. And when Shana arrived on the scene of a domestic disturbance or drive-by shooting and children were involved, it ripped her heart right out of her chest. She had taken her oath as a police officer to preserve, protect, and defend the public, but once on the job, she found herself taking extra care to shelter the children from the shit storm of many of their lives. She guessed that it stemmed from her own childhood.

••••••

If I can best describe my household growing up as strained, particularly during my teenaged years, Shana says hers took that next dysfunctional step into mayhem. Between her father's long addiction to marijuana and alcohol and her mother's apparent emotional imbalance, Shana and her younger sister were often left to fend for themselves. There were periods of time when Shana's grandparents had to come once a week to put food in the refrigerator and do a load of laundry just so she and her sister, Alyssa, would have something to eat and clothes for school.

Shana was raised in a string of working-class towns on the south shore of Long Island, New York, and her earliest memory is of running away from home when she was about four years old. After packing her red wagon with her most precious toys, she headed out of the house and down the street, looking over her shoulder to see if her parents were coming after her to bring her home. They weren't. A few houses down the street, she got nervous and tucked behind a row of bushes, peeking out to see if her parents were coming yet. Surely by now they were crazy with worry and guilt for having forced their tiny daughter out of the house and down the street? Nope. The street was empty, and she was alone. After sitting under the bushes for what felt like three hours but was probably closer to three minutes, awaiting a frantic search party of loving and repentant parents that never came, Shana turned around and slowly pulled her wagon back home, her head hanging low. She never forgot that sense of feeling invisible to her parents and alone in the world.

During her parents' protracted six-year separation and eventual nasty divorce, Shana's home became outright chaotic. Even before her father left, theirs was known by neighbors as the "crazy" house where at times the police were called after bouts of screaming. Once her father had moved out for good when Shana was ten, it became her unofficial job to take care of things: the house, Alyssa, and her increasingly erratic mother. Shana was the one who mowed the lawn when the grass needed cutting, shoveled the driveway when it snowed, and made sure the pipes didn't freeze on frigid winter nights. When their father would pull into the driveway to see Shana and her sister, their mother would start screaming profanity-laced accusations. Always the peacemaker in the turbulent house, it was Shana who calmed everybody down and sent the summoned cops on their way, assuring them, "Everything is all right, officers." But what she remembered about those visits, even as a young girl, was feeling dismissed or even ignored by the police when she tried to explain what was happening in the house and who had caused the commotion. She wanted to yell at them, *Hey! I'm the sober one here! Listen to me!* Instead she was usually brushed aside rather than being offered support or protection, and she made a silent vow that if she was ever in that position, she would hear the kids out and at the very least let them know that their version of the story mattered. When the turmoil around her father's visits increased, he was finally forced to stay away entirely, but to Shana, it felt as if he had *chosen* to stay away. It took her years to understand and forgive the hurt and to rebuild her relationship with him.

●●●●●●

Even with all of what she calls the "crazy town" of a dysfunctional mother, to say nothing of her multiple and at times abusive boyfriends, Shana still has some funny, even fond, memories of growing up, but they most often involve her kid sister. Alyssa was born four and half years after Shana, and in many ways they became each other's salvation, if at times somewhat bruised and abused saviors. Alyssa remembers the time she unwisely taunted Shana into wrestling and soon found herself flat on the kitchen floor, arms and legs tightly pinned, while Shana used her free arm to open the fridge door, grab the ketchup bottle from the bottom shelf, and pour it all over Alyssa's face. Shana then called in the family dog to lick Alyssa's face clean. Not only bigger in years and size, Shana often stepped in as the unofficial parent, the one who made sure Alyssa didn't cross any lines as they got older. One afternoon when Alyssa was twelve, she invited boys to come home from school to play with her and her friend Claire. Shana surprised the little gathering by arriving home unexpectedly early from high school and promptly threw the boys out, telling them to "get the hell out of here before I call your mothers!" As the startled boys scrambled to the side of the house where they had left their bicycles, they were shocked to find them gone and even more shocked when they spied their bikes floating in the nearby river, where Shana had dumped them. Her only words to Alyssa before retreating to her room to do homework were "You know the rules. No boys in the house unless I'm home."

Shana was fifteen when the World Trade Center towers came down. Not only was Lower Manhattan only forty miles west of their house but her father was working a construction job that day in an office near the Queens Midtown Tunnel, less than four miles from Ground Zero. To Shana, and untold millions of fellow New Yorkers, the attacks felt personal. Terrorist bombings in the Middle East were one thing, but to those close enough to smell the smoke and see the ash blowing between the buildings of lower Manhattan, it was another thing entirely. Without knowing it, that feeling of having no control over the mayhem found root in her psyche, and the urge to fight back against it only grew stronger as she matured. She might not be able to control jihadist nuts bent on suicide missions, but damn if she wasn't going to do her part to keep them as far from her streets as possible.

When she graduated with honors from Connetquot High School in Bohemia, New York, Shana knew she had to forever escape the small town *and* her mother. She had known for years that she was gay, but as she got older, she knew it would be impossible to live that truth and survive anywhere near her mother. Her determination to never, ever return to Bayshore, New York, had pushed her to achieve, and in the fall, she started at Northeastern University in Boston.

It was during her third year at Northeastern, with a solid GPA but no solid plans, that she suddenly stumbled upon what would be her path. Walking through the Student Union one day, she saw a notice of the Boston Police Department's upcoming annual civil service exam. Following her father's motto of "Take every test" because tests can open unknown doors, she took it, aced it, and was soon invited in for an impossibly hard-to-get interview with the department. The timing couldn't have been worse. Days before her scheduled interview, she had been admitted to the hospital with acute diverticulitis so bad that she had to be on a morphine drip for the pain. But she would not be deterred. She threatened the on-duty nurse that she would "rip these fucking IV tubes out right now" if she wasn't released and allowed to go to her interview. Thankfully, before she could do that, her luck changed. It turned out that the nurse's father worked in the police department's recruitment unit, and with a quick phone call, Shana's interview was rescheduled.

The interview was ultimately a great success, and she was accepted onto the force. One of the recruiters during her interview told her that he was sick of all the straight white status quo men around and that they needed "more people like you." Shana didn't know if he was referring to her being a woman or to her being an openly gay woman, and she didn't care. She wanted in, and she got in. She finished her fourth year at Northeastern but opted not to complete her fifth and final year (Northeastern University has a five-year degree plan, allowing students to spend at least one of those years actively engaged in their chosen major) and instead entered the Boston Police Academy's eight-hundred-hour, twenty-four-week training program in the spring of 2008.

Upon graduation, she was assigned to the rather upscale West Roxbury neighborhood of Boston, about five miles south of Boston proper. But instead of a public servant to those who needed protecting, she felt more like a babysitter to the rich and privileged. After a routine probationary period, she asked to be transferred to another neighborhood. Although it was only a few miles east, Roxbury proper was another world in terms of violent crime and pervasive danger. In short order, the rookie cop from Long Island was responding to calls on drive-by gang shootings, dead junkies on benches, wives and prostitutes beaten black and blue, babies left for dead on front stoops, suicides and suicide threats, and all manner of rages, fits, and fights among "booze bags" and drug addicts. But she loved her job. Being able to help, to even save lives when necessary, made her proud to wear the blue uniform. Being able to protect terrified women and too often children. Being one of the good guys in bad situations. Being a Boston cop. It didn't take long before she couldn't imagine doing anything else.

On April 15, 2013, Shana was scheduled to be off duty but readily volunteered to work an extra shift. Not only was Marathon Monday a fun day to work, it was also a state holiday and therefore double pay—something she rarely, if ever, turned down. Plus, she loved working the marathon. Everybody was friendly, most of them obeyed the rules and stayed on their side of the barricade, and a terrific free lunch was served in the Lenox Hotel to almost all of the uniforms working the crowd, courtesy of the Boston Athletic Association. She reported to work for her shift, found she'd be patrolling the Boston Common, and switched assignments so she could work the much more exciting position along the finish line. It was a gorgeous day, sunny and calm and a bit chilly, so Shana wore her heavy ski gloves to keep her perpetually cold fingers warm. The crowds were behaving for the most part—there were just a few who had had one drink too many in nearby bars—and Shana was able to relax and enjoy the day, even stopping along the barricade to smile into the camera of a friend who was strolling the sidewalk on Boylston Street.

When the first bomb went off at 2:49 p.m., Shana was only about a hundred feet away. Like many people on the scene, she didn't know what it was at first. She felt rattled, like she'd been shaken hard. She saw the smoke but didn't see the grisly scene on the other side of the barricade and the blood pooling on the sidewalk underneath Krystle Campbell, Jeff Bauman, Mery Daniel, Celeste Corcoran, and many others, some of whom lost their lives and others their limbs when the first pressure cooker filled with BBs, screws, and nails exploded inches from where they stood. Shana pulled her gun and ran to the middle of Boylston Street, trying to calm her brain and force it into emergency reaction mode: *Find cover and assess. Breathe.* She, along with almost every cop and firefighter anywhere near Boylston Street that day, had the same thought at that moment: if this is a bomb, the terrorists aren't aiming for civilians and runners along a marathon route—*they are aiming for us.*

Find cover and assess. Breathe.

Shana circled around in the middle of the street with her gun drawn, like Wyatt Earp in the O.K. Corral. But she barely had time to pivot once before the second blast was heard and felt two hundred yards up Boylston Street.

Shana told me she doesn't know what happened next, and probably never will. One thing is clear, although she has no memory of it: she ran. With the smoke from the first bomb burning in her lungs and the smoke from the second bomb billowing toward her, she ran into that second cloud. She doesn't know how long it took her to run the two football fields toward me, but what she remembers next is seeing me lying in the middle of an odd huddle in the middle of the street, a young white kid kneeling on my right side struggling with a belt tourniquet and a middle-aged black man kneeling on the other side, holding my hand. She saw that they were struggling to keep one of the mortally wounded victims alive. That jolted everything back into focus, and Officer Shana Cottone was again on high alert.

She ran over, knelt down, and crouched low over my face, a bit too close for my comfort, but I didn't know then that she had a purpose in practically coming in nose to nose. She reached out and took my right hand, and I held on, grateful that she somehow knew that that simple gesture was what I needed most—aside from an ambulance and a heavy dose of morphine, of course.

Shana tells me she could deal with other people's blood all day on the job, but her own? Forget about it. In fact, she passes out nine times out of ten when she gives blood. So the last thing she wanted was for me to look down at my ruined leg. She knew how bad it was because she was looking right at it. She was afraid if I saw it I'd puke or pass out or both, and then she'd have a whole other set of problems on her hands.

She was right. One of the few saving graces of that day was that I never saw my own ruined leg. Even later, when I was offered an opportunity to look at the presurgery pictures taken in the operating room before my amputation, I refused. It's gone. No use staring at the ruination. Lying there, I knew it was bad, but I didn't know yet quite how bad.

Shana began talking to me. "I'm a police officer. My name is Shana. You're gonna be all right. What's your name?"

"Roseann, Roseann Sdoia."

"Were you watching your husband run?"

"What the hell does that have to do with anything?"

She still has some life in her, Shana thought, but she didn't know how that was possible, given how much blood I'd lost. What she didn't like was that the tourniquet was not tight enough on my leg, and she told the kid to pull harder. He did. I screamed and suddenly heard my friend Alissa shrieking, "Oh, my GOD! It's Roseann!" as she recognized me lying on the street.

When I was able to give Alissa Gia's phone number without having to think twice about what the number was, Shana was again relieved. Not only did it stop Alissa's screaming, but if victims can coherently provide information, their brains are still functioning. If their brains are still functioning, they haven't begun the disastrous slide into shock—shock that shuts the body down piece by piece, trying to save its core.

As Alissa stepped away from the huddle to call Gia, all I heard was sirens, presumably police cars and ambulances, but none, it seemed, were coming for me. Time after time, one would approach, even slow down, but then its screeching wail would fade off.

Above me, I could feel that Officer Cottone was getting more and more desperate and angry. At one point she pulled her hand from mine, and I heard her yell, "I don't give a fuck if you're full; we need to load her now! She'll die right here if we don't."

But I guess they too drove away because Shana came back and again took my hand.

After what seemed like a month, I finally heard tires screech to a stop, voices yelling to "Grab the head!" and "Load and go!" and I felt my backboard lift off the street.

Shana let go of my hand and watched the group of firefighters lift me into the back of the wagon.

"Let's GO!" I heard Shana yell as she banged on the wall of the paddy wagon before jumping into the front with Davis. But no sooner had her front door slammed than I heard her yell, "FUCK!" and jump back out, run around to the back, and slam the door, which had remained open.

My pain and panic were finally relieved by a degree when I felt the van move beneath me; with that movement came the blessed relief that soon I would be in a hospital, in the best medical hands in the Northern Hemisphere, and on a morphine drip. But mostly I was thankful to be off that godforsaken pavement and away from the bombs that had torn Boston apart, and with it my leg.

In the cab, Shana wasn't feeling anything close to relief. She still felt as if her head was in a vat of thick mud, both suffocating and dulling. She wondered if she'd ever have a clear thought again. Fear that she was going to die still raced through her veins and stomach like boiling tar, but she was also weirdly numb, like coming out from under anesthesia. Like many trained first responders, she pushed down her rising panic and forced herself to focus on the world outside the windshield. When she did, her fear turned instantly to frustration—the paddy wagon could barely move through the milling crowds; people were moving like zombies through the same mud in which she seemed to move. She pulled the van's PA mic out of its cradle on the dash so hard that its cord nearly detached from the radio. She hit the transmit button, which immediately stopped the siren.

"Shit!"

Jim Davis looked over unapologetically and shrugged. "This van's from the Carter administration. Can't use the siren and the PA at once."

"FUCK!" Shana screamed but nonetheless hit "transmit" and silenced the siren above them.

"THIS IS THE BOSTON POLICE. MOVE OUT OF THE WAY. NOW!"

The zombies barely budged. She turned the siren back on and resorted to her tried-and-true method of communication: she rolled down the window and hung nearly halfway out of it, screaming over the siren, "GET THE FUCK OUT OF THE WAY! MOVE!"

Officer Davis concentrated on the road, mindful of his payload. He had a little over two miles to cover through some of Boston's narrowest streets and tightest corners, so he tempered his tendency to drive with a lead foot. He also was dealing with his increasingly frantic colleague on the seat next to him. He recognized that Shana was rushing with adrenaline and in danger of falling out of the window as she yelled at pedestrians. As he neared a particularly tight corner, Davis reached out with his right hand and pulled her back into the cab by her gun belt before she fell out. He felt a measure of almost paternal pride: *Damn, this woman can yell! She is almost as loud as the siren.*

Shana sat back in her seat. Screaming at the crowds hadn't calmed her down and it certainly didn't help move the dopey idiots out of the way, but it had felt oddly satisfying to give voice to her terror and frustration. She took a deep breath, let Davis drive his van, and watched the scene unfolding in front of her. It was a sea of people moving in all directions, none hurriedly anymore; the bombs had gone off over twenty-five minutes before. Now people were just milling around, wondering at the chaos and the fact that they were able to walk down the middle of a usually busy downtown Boston street.

Her relative calm lasted exactly ten seconds. Unable to sit still another second, she again unrolled her window and hung out of the paddy wagon.

"Fucking MOVE, you idiots or I'll get out and move you myself!" It wasn't exactly her finest hour as an ambassador for Boston's men and women in blue.

Shana was also trying to talk Davis out of going to Mass General Hospital. She had a panic-fueled and totally irrational notion that the drive from Boylston Street to Mass General involved going through a tunnel. It didn't, but in her mind it did, and she was sure that a tunnel was where she would meet her doom. The sense of being trapped and powerless again, particularly in a tunnel, felt like hands around her throat. *I bet terrorists love tunnels*, she thought. *Close off one side, get the emergency vehicle to enter, and boom, you have another whole cast of trapped, dead characters.*

Thankfully, Davis would hear none of it. He was taking his patients to Mass General for one simple reason: he considered it the best trauma unit in the city. Skirting through the narrow streets he'd been driving his whole life, knowing where to avoid the worst of the traffic, and driving on the left-hand side of the street when cars impeded his progress on the right, Davis drove behind Boylston, through the Boston Common, up and over Beacon Hill, and finally down the other side toward MGH.

As we slowed at what I could only hope and pray was the hospital, I heard people banging on the outside of the van.

"Clear that paddy wagon out of here! We have multiple traumas coming in!"

Davis ignored them and backed the van to and practically *through* the emergency doors. Before the van stopped, Shana was out of the vehicle. One of the ER docs tried one more time: "Officer, get that van out of here! We have incoming casualties."

"Two of them are right here," she shot back and opened the van's rear doors.

ER doctors, and especially large-city ER doctors, have seen a lot of blood, mangled bodies, DOA accident victims, and countless other forms of wrecked and wretched humanity come through their doors. But no one had experienced what they saw when Shana opened the police-van doors. Usually when a police vehicle comes into emergency, it's because a drunk needs his stomach pumped or a drug addict has overdosed or a gang member needs a few stitches after a street fight—otherwise they'd arrive in an ambulance. But in this van were two firefighters in full bunker gear kneeling on the floor, each crouched over a bench, one hand braced on the wall, the other gripped on some sort of tourniquet, the sheer bulk of their bodies holding the patients on backboards in place against the walls. The grisly tableau was awash in blood. Because Marc and I had been put headfirst in the van, from where the doctors stood by the doors, all they could see of him and me were the gnarled remains of our legs.

"Oh, my God!" I heard someone exclaim. "They're bringing them in in paddy wagons!"

Yup, I wanted to say, *and thank God!*

Mike took the head of my board, and ER personnel took the foot, and they carried me out of the van and into the hospital. Finally.

It was 3:22 p.m., just over thirty minutes after the bombs. I was one of the last to arrive at the hospital. I had lost 3.5 liters of blood, nearly 90 percent of my total blood volume. At the rate I was bleeding, I had about five minutes to live. I had stayed awake through it all, determined to survive. As they placed me on the hospital gurney, I finally let go.

Let someone else be in charge of whether I live or die was my last cognitive thought before I let myself slip into unconsciousness and away from the pain.

Nearly an hour after the bombs and when I was stabilized, they wheeled me into surgery. As crazy as it sounds, there were still people running the marathon back in the suburbs who hadn't yet learned what lay miles ahead of them on Boylston Street.

If not for Shores Salter holding the tourniquet, Officer Shana Cottone making sure I didn't die right there on the pavement, and firefighter Mike Materia assuring that I survived the trip to Mass General, I would have been among those who didn't make it off the pavement alive.

I was one of the lucky ones that day.

······

As they wheeled me away from the emergency bay, Shana wasn't feeling lucky at all. The van's police radio had crackled to life, and with it orders to head back to Boylston Street. The emergency circuits were jammed with reports of panicked citizens calling about possible bomb sightings all over town—the JFK

Library in Dorchester, the lobby of the Lenox Hotel, and in front of Abe & Louie's Grill, both a few doors down from the Forum on Boylston. In the midst of the cacophony, Officer Davis got a call to pick up a four-man bomb squad and escort them around to follow up on the latest sightings.

With a sickening jolt, she realized they had to go back to Ground Zero. Bending behind the van, she doubled over and vomited. When she had emptied her stomach, she wiped her mouth, straightened her back, and looked up as Materia and Foley emerged from the emergency doors, their coats, pants, and boots blotched with blood, their hands covered with it.

"You okay?" Mike asked.

Shana, embarrassed at her show of weakness and fear, nodded but said nothing.

"Okay! Let's load 'em up," Davis called from the cab. "We're headed back."

Mike and Pat Foley climbed back into the fetid metal box.

"Please leave one of the doors open. We're dyin' back here," Mike pleaded with Shana, who obliged, shutting the interior cage doors but leaving one of the outer steel doors loose, allowing Mike and Pat at least some light, if not exactly fresh air, for the drive back to Boylston Street.

Shana was grateful that she could ride up front, particularly with her now untrustworthy stomach. Even on a good day, she suffered from debilitating carsickness, and today was *not* a good day. Better to have a window to puke out of.

As the van made its way out of the hospital's emergency bay, she pulled out her phone and punched a number in her favorites. Unlike many other calls that afternoon, this one rang through.

"Dad," she said, struggling with the words and tears that choked her, "there's been an attack. I don't know what is going on, but I'm okay, and I love you."

She didn't tell her father, but she thought it might be the last time she ever spoke to him; she was that sure they were headed into another attack.

She hung up before she lost it in front of Officer Davis. It was just the kind of show of weakness she'd never live down at the station house. But hearing her father's voice was so power-ful, so painful, that she had to end the call fast. She turned her face away from Davis and wiped a lone tear from her cheek, trying to focus on the world outside her window.

Before picking up the bomb squad, they first had to get their firefighters, who by now were banging on the inside of the van to be released from the blood-soaked and reeking van, back to Boylston Street. When the van stopped, Shana went back and opened the cage doors, and Pat and Mike stumbled out. Mike took his first deep breath in what felt like years. Even with one door open, it still stank to high heaven.

"Jesus! Do you guys ever clean these things?" he asked, the stench of the metal box wafting thickly off his clothing.

Shana ignored him, closed the doors, and silently climbed back into the cab with Davis. Without opening it to discus-sion, Shana had made the decision to stick with Davis and his paddy wagon. She hadn't heard a word from her station chief since the bombing—she didn't even know if they knew whether she was alive or dead. Besides, she felt safer with Davis in the van, and safer still after they picked up the bomb squad to respond to calls and to protect the evidence, body parts, and even the bodies, still lying in puddles of blood on the bricks and cement, for examination by the FBI. It was still an active crime scene.

When the men from the bomb squad climbed into the back, they were a little more diplomatic than Mike had been, asking, "What is that *smell*?"

••••••

Davis parked the van on the corner of Boylston and Exeter Streets while the bomb squad checked out a couple of reports near Forum. On the street a few feet in front of them, he saw a foot in a sneaker zipped into a plastic bag with a bright yellow tag next to it. The evidence gathering had begun. Half a block up the street toward Forum, it was eerily empty except for two bodies near a green mailbox, both draped in restaurant table-cloths. Two police officers stood guard.

For the rest of the late afternoon and evening, Shana rode with Davis and the bomb squad, following up on radio calls about possible bomb sightings and suspicious packages spotted in different parts of the city. Wherever they went, they encountered the same scene: people milling about with an odd detachment. It reminded Shana of a middle-of-the-night fire alarm with the hotel guests or apartment-building residents, still half asleep, wandering about glassy-eyed, awaiting instructions on when they can get back to their rooms and to bed. Some people were horrified, and others were merely annoyed. A few people approached Shana and Davis and asked when they could get beyond the barricades and claim their marathon towel or find their running bag. Shana wanted to yell in their clueless faces that people had died, their blood still stained the pavement, *and you want your fucking towel?* She held her tongue. Well, mostly.

She admits she let a few profane comments fly that she regrets, given that she was, after all, in uniform.

At close to 11:00 p.m., Davis said he was calling it a night and heading back to his station. She thanked him and hopped out near where she had parked her car. She felt like it had been a year since she had parked there, though it had been less than a day. She headed home. As she drove through streets notorious for their violent crime, she had never felt safer in her life. With every block she put between herself and Boylston Street, she felt the adrenaline that had been coursing through her veins for nearly nine hours finally begin to fade. She could focus again. She could breathe.

By the time she finally made it back to her house in Hyde Park sometime after midnight, she had been on her feet for close to twenty hours. She had held the hand of one of those critically injured in the bombing. She had returned to the bloody streets, protecting the evidence and the bodies for FBI investigators. She had assisted emergency crews and the bomb squad. And she had held it together, for the most part. But when she finally put her key in her door and saw Monkey, her beloved beagle, waiting for her with his anxious, sweet eyes, she fell apart. Gathering the pup into her arms, she walked into her living room, nestled into the couch cushions with him, put her face into his warm neck, and sobbed.

chapter six

AWAKE

I WAS AWAKE. Standing at my bedside were Mom, Dad, Gia, and a handsome doctor in a white coat. Groggy from the anesthesia and pain medications, I had no idea it was already Tuesday evening. I had lost, along with most of my blood and the lower half of my right leg, a day and a half of my life.

Dad looked like he'd aged years. Mom smiled at me with tears and terror in her eyes. I could tell she was dying for a cigarette. Then again, she was always dying for a cigarette. The doctor wore the weary smile of someone who has seen too much.

"Hi, Roseann, I'm Dr. King."

As freakishly unlucky as I had been to find myself inches away from a bomb, I was incredibly lucky that Dr. David King awaited the victims in Mass General Hospital's trauma bay. A surgical veteran of the Iraq and Afghanistan wars as well as the Haitian earthquake relief efforts, Dr. King had been in a cab driving back to his home in Cambridge after running the marathon himself when the first texts came in to his cell phone: "Are you ok?" "Heard there was an explosion!" "Bomb at Marathon? Have you finished the race?" "Hope you are safe!" "R U still running?"

King had dropped his wife and two young daughters at home and immediately headed straight to Mass General, less than a mile away across the Charles River. When he pulled up to the ambulance ramp, he almost turned around and went home: everything looked normal, even quiet. There were no screaming ambulances, no police cruisers, no crush of nurses and doctors at the emergency-room doors. But he just had a feeling. With the hair on the back of his neck standing on end, he thought, *What the hell, I'm here. I'd better go have a look.*

Even though he had just run 26.2 miles in just over three hours, he ran up three flights of stairs to grab his surgical scrub cap and protective operating glasses. No matter what awaited him in the ER, he wanted to be able to get right to work. He hurried back down the stairs to the ER.

King didn't yet know what the nature of the explosion had been: industrial accident, propane tank, gas line—but as soon as he walked through the ER doors and saw the beds crowded with bloodied victims, he knew: *These people have been blown up by an IED.*

The pattern of a bomb blast is unique, not only to its victims but to the shape of the blast itself. Essentially, no two bombs are alike, and no two people are injured in the same way. The bombs that took not just my leg but eventually another nineteen legs from sixteen other victims were made with pressure cookers filled with gunpowder, BBs, nails, and screws. Unlike a professionally made bomb with military-grade components that explode in a uniform blast, these "improvised" and amateur bombs exploded in a thousand different directions. It was

entirely dumb luck that at the scene of the first bomb, Jeff Bauman lost both legs above the knee in a fraction of a second while
a woman to his right suffered only minor hearing damage. In my
case, the second bomb, which killed two people less than ten
feet away from me, "only" took my right leg.

As the most critically injured in the blasts made their way to
the four closest trauma units in Boston, doctors receiving them
knew two things: that they were soon to be overrun with untold
numbers of mortally wounded patients and that the culprit had
been some sort of explosion on Boylston Street. For King, once
he saw the victims, there was a third realization. Few American
doctors have seen the reality of war and its ability to produce
hundreds of wounded in an instant. Even fewer have seen the
relatively recent influx of IEDs into everyday battle and the catastrophic damage they inflict on the human body. He was one
of the few who'd seen both. One of the many mind-numbing
realizations that would occur to King in the coming days was
that America had just suffered its first major modern terrorist
event resulting in mass trauma with warlike lower-extremity injuries. Never before had hundreds of Americans been blown up
by ground-level bombs. This, he knew, was a devastating milestone in the nation's history.

When they moved me into the ER, Francis McNulty, RN,
was on duty. Until 3:00 p.m., his shift in the emergency room
had been normal, and about sixteen of the trauma-bay beds had
patients awaiting evaluation. Then the ER received a call to expect mass casualties: the staff members weren't told what had
happened but were instructed to clear every possible bed for
incoming victims. Miraculously, that happened within minutes.
Wow. I wish we could clear patients that fast every day, McNulty
thought. Then all hell broke loose. At 3:04, the first patients

arrived, and soon after, the ER became a sea of trauma wounds. As McNulty focused on the first of the injured coming into the emergency department, he heard rather than saw the doors to the trauma bay repeatedly banging open and with them the screams of the wounded, EMS crews hurriedly reciting their patients' stats and handing them off, and nurses and doctors calling for IVs and X-rays, chest tubes and tourniquets. In less than twenty-five minutes, Mass General received thirty-one victims from the bombing, five of whom would lose their legs. McNulty went as quickly as he could from bed to bed, checking the patients' vitals and trying to get them stable for transport to the operating room. As he did, he appreciated that as ugly and bloody as trauma wounds were, unlike infections or diseases, where an untold number of calamities and dangers lurk just beneath the surface, the initial treatment was simple and straightforward: stop the bleeding, stabilize the breathing, get the patients on a unit of blood, and send them upstairs for surgery. But there was one thing about these patients that wasn't at all routine. McNulty found himself staring at tiny gold nails, like the ones you hang pictures with, lying on the sheets next to some of the wounded. Shiny and new-looking, they just lay there, not bloody or embedded in legs or arms. McNulty figured they had been intended as shrapnel, along with the BBs and screws, but instead had just gotten tangled in these patients' clothing or hair. Unlike the other ingredients in the bombs, these nails had miraculously not done any harm.

McNulty looked up from the odd little nails and saw a man in the next bed talking on his cell phone. McNulty was struck by how calm he was, given that one of his legs was all but gone below the knee. McNulty wondered if it could even be saved.

"Honey," the man said calmly into the phone, "be sure to walk the dog. I won't be home in time to do it."

Dude, screw the dog, McNulty thought. *Your leg is gone.* Realizing that the man was not calm so much as he was in shock, McNulty took the phone from him and said to the woman at the other end, "You'd better get over here. He is not going to die, but he's been injured, and you need to come."

He stabilized the man's tourniquet and moved on. As he did, he saw a large firefighter in full bunker gear holding an improvised tourniquet on a woman's leg and helping push her into the room on a gurney.

"Bring her over here," McNulty told Mike.

As they wheeled me into trauma bay 12, McNulty asked Mike what had happened. He was well aware that firefighters don't usually have the onerous task of bringing the mortally wounded into the ER and relaying life-and-death information to the doctors and nurses; usually firefighters apply lifesaving triage at the scene, then hand off the critical care to the ambulance EMTs. But there had been no EMTs in the back of that paddy wagon, and Mike did his best to give McNulty every piece of crucial information he could: ground-level blast, right leg severely damaged, improvised tourniquet applied on the street, minor burns to right arm and hand, patient alert and verbal. "But other than that," Mike told McNulty, "all we could do was 'scoop and run.' Sorry."

"Good enough, man. Good job," McNulty told Mike as he instructed an orderly to take control of the tourniquet and began assessing my injuries.

McNulty looked down at me and saw many things all at once: the inadequate tourniquet, the mess of my right leg in the splint, the burns and shrapnel wounds to my left leg and arms, and that my face was the color of ashes. He immediately went to work getting me stable for surgery. He never saw the firefighter leave.

McNulty says I looked up at him then, my eyes full of fear and questions. I don't remember any of it, or that I was ever conscious in the ER.

"Your leg is pretty bad," he told me, experience having taught him that sugarcoating a critical injury is pointless. Shock or no shock, the patients usually know better than anybody how hurt they are. "But you're in the best place possible, and we're going to take care of you."

Even though I don't remember the exchange, he says I nodded and again closed my eyes, shutting out the activity around me.

Knowing he had to get an IV in my arm and hoping to God my veins hadn't collapsed with the loss of blood pressure, McNulty scolded an orderly who had started to remove the splint from my leg.

"Stop!" McNulty shouted. "I need to get the IV in before we release the leg from the splint." Otherwise, he knew, I would continue to bleed out.

After he had successfully inserted the IV needle into my arm and the first units of replacement blood were safely coursing through my body, Dr. King came into the trauma bay.

When he saw me, he could see that my wound was exsanguinating—losing so much blood so fast that he could hear it gushing. He also realized that if he couldn't stop the bleeding within minutes, I'd be dead. King estimated that nearly my entire blood volume, every red blood cell I owned, had been left somewhere on Boylston Street or in the paddy wagon, and now in the ER. Because I was the closest patient to him in the trauma bay, he hurried over and quickly replaced the now slick and flimsy belt tourniquet with a proper locking CAT device.

Moving with the no-nonsense efficiency of a battlefield surgeon, King evaluated my obvious wound and made sure the tourniquet was applied securely. Then he and McNulty turned me over so he could inspect my back; he wanted to make sure there was no wound or internal bleeding that people had missed in the chaos. He knew those hidden injuries are snakes in the grass that often end up killing a patient because they go ignored for too long. While my back was clear of wounds and bruises, as my clothes were cut away, they saw a troubling blue contusion across my belly, which King didn't like the looks of at all. Because there was no open wound, he feared it might indicate internal damage to any number of organs: stomach, spleen, liver, or kidneys. He knew that with my leg now stabilized, getting into my abdominal cavity would be his first order of business in the operating room. With his surgical plan in place, he ordered a chest X-ray, checked on the blood supply hanging above my gurney, and called ahead to the OR to say that he and I were on our way. It all took about ninety seconds.

Meanwhile, McNulty removed the splint from my right leg and, sure enough, watched what was left of the leg fall apart before his eyes. McNulty was impressed that the firefighters had been able to get the splint on my leg in the first place, given that it was such a mess.

McNulty and King say I was awake during this time, quiet, pale, and teary-eyed. "Please, Doctor, don't let me die," I said to Dr. King. He nodded and continued his pre-op calculations.

And even after all of my prayers for morphine while lying on Boylston Street and in the paddy wagon, once McNulty finally offered me some, I evidently said I wasn't in much pain.

McNulty figured it was most likely the shock talking and administered a shot anyway. Thank God!

••••••

By Tuesday evening, Dr. King had determined that I was out of the woods and that it was time to bring me out of controlled sedation. He had put me in the so-called induced coma so that my body could recover from the immediate shock to the system and to help me tolerate the plastic tube stuck down my throat to help me breathe.

Now Dr. King stood over my bed, introducing himself. I nodded back at him, not sure whether I could even talk. My mouth felt as if I'd been eating sawdust mixed with sand for a week.

As I slowly came out from under the weight of sedation, King was giving me the barest facts: I had been hurt, I had been brought to Mass General (*that* much I knew—in fact, I remembered that I had insisted on it), and he had had to amputate my right leg below the knee. Again, it wasn't a shock; I knew I'd lost the lower leg way back on Boylston Street. What he was careful not to tell me was *how* I had been hurt. He felt that bit of news needed to come from a loved one.

I struggled to clear what felt like a cotton ball out of my mouth in order to speak.

"Well, at least I'm alive."

King made a mental note: *This one's going to be fine.* After performing thousands of amputations, he had become deft at recognizing those patients who would quickly pick up the pieces and move on with their lives versus those who never regained their emotional, to say nothing of physical, balance. He knew I would be okay. He gave me a quick nod of approval and left the room to continue his rounds.

I looked at Mom and felt a tear drip down my cheek. Funny how seeing our mothers when we are at our most vulnerable touches something deep in our hearts. But I allowed just one tear. The last thing I wanted was for her to scold me for crying.

"I don't want any pity," I told her. "I couldn't stand it if people felt sorry for me."

"Have I ever pitied you before?" she said. "Why would I start now?"

God love her. It was Mom at her maternal best.

I realized that Gia and Dad were in the room as well, and I looked from face to face, trying to figure it all out through the thick haze of morphine. I moved my tongue around in my mouth and opened my dry lips, which cracked with the effort.

"Fuck. It is what it is," I said, not really sure to this day why I said it. First of all, I rarely use the word "fuck." Second, I hate that saying, "It is what it is." It's such a cop-out. Such a lazy answer to a problem, usually one that does in fact have a solution. "It is what it is." *No, it's NOT*, I always wanted to yell at the person. *You can try to fix it, you can make it better, you can at least make an attempt.*

But as I clawed my way out of the heavy anesthesia fog, I said it. And in this case, it was true. There was no changing it or solving this problem. The leg was gone. *It is what it is.* My awareness of losing my leg came and went with the doses of painkiller, but I knew it was bad enough for Mom to look oddly nervous and Gia to look stricken with worry and exhaustion.

"And I thought turning forty-five was bad," I said to her.

Gia laughed, as I hoped she would. My forty-fifth birthday in March had been a tough one for me, and Gia knew it better than anybody.

Gia, Mom, Dad, and my Aunt Paula had been there since getting the terrible call and had tried not to gasp out loud when they had first seen me in the ICU bed. My face, nose, and lips were burned, like a chemical peel gone terribly, terribly wrong; my eyebrows were singed off; my hair was a stiff Brillo pad sticking straight up on my head; and tubes were coming out of seemingly every inch of my body. But as bad as I looked, once Gia saw me, she knew I would live. "You're a fighter, Roseann," she told me later. "I knew if you'd lived through the bombing, you'd make it."

I looked up at Mom, scared to ask what had been haunting me since I'd awakened.

"Are Megan and Sabrina okay?" I remembered Jenna and Alissa from the street. (How could I forget Alissa and that screaming?) But Megan and Sabrina had disappeared, and I feared the worst. Sabrina had been only inches away from me at the mailbox.

Mom reached out and gave my arm a few pats, the limits of her touchy-feely reassurances.

"Yes, they're fine. They've been waiting to see you."

Reassured for the moment but not entirely convinced, I lay back and allowed myself to sink again into the painkiller fog.

Somewhere in the chaos of the bombing and the jumble of my immediate thoughts as I lay on Boylston Street, I had wondered, *Why did someone throw a grenade at me?* I thought *I* was the target. I had no idea I was one of tens of thousands of targets. In one of those early moments of fleeting consciousness in the hospital, I looked up at Mom and said, "I didn't do anything."

I thought it was about me.

••••••

In the coming weeks, I would hear everybody's various "where I was when I heard the news" story, but I heard Mom's first.

"Oh, my God, Roseann," she began, her hand reflexively reaching for her purse to get a storytelling cigarette before remembering where she was, "I was in the garden when my cell phone rang."

After telling Mom that I had been hurt in an explosion at the marathon and that she was on her way to pick her up, Gia had allowed only the briefest of chilling fear to sweep through her body before shaking herself back into action. She grabbed her keys, headed for her car, and called Patrick to say she was headed to get Mom and then into Boston to find me.

At his end of the call, Patrick wasn't wild about her heading into what was clearly a war zone, with two bombs already detonated and God only knew how many more. But as he started to voice his protest, Gia quickly silenced him.

"Patrick. Ro may have lost a leg. I'm going."

He then shut up, realizing he was powerless against Gia's almost animal need to find her wounded sister. "Okay, hon. Just be careful."

"I will. Go get Jessica at her softball game. I don't want her finding out about her aunt from some damn tweet or text."

Gia and Patrick's three girls are as much my daughters as they are my nieces. When Jane, my first niece, was born, I was living in Florida and couldn't get back to Boston in time for the delivery. Frantic for news, I called the nurse's station at the hospital every two minutes (I'm not exaggerating—I called every two minutes) so that I got the news that Jane had been born before all the grandparents who were right there in the waiting room did. I'm the textbook doting aunt to those three girls, and in return they give me all the unconditional love and affection any aunt could desire.

Gia and Patrick both knew that telling the girls I was gravely wounded would be one of the hardest things they had ever done. When Patrick approached Jessica at her softball game, she looked up from her phone, her face frozen in panic and anguish, and he knew he was too late. Her older sister, Jane, had seen news of the bombings on television, then learned from her mother that I had been hurt. She had tweeted that I was injured, and a flurry of their friends had immediately started texting, offering prayers and support. Silently, Patrick wrapped his daughter in his arms, and they stood together on the edge of the field, crying.

In all of the horrible "what ifs" of the bombing, one is that my mother and three nieces could have been in the middle of it all. On and off for years, they made it a date to go into Boston on Marathon Monday and stand on Boylston Street to watch the runners cross the finish line. Their prime viewing spot was in front of Uno Pizzeria at 731 Boylston—exactly halfway between where the first and second bombs exploded. But the Friday before, Mom had told me they wouldn't be going in this year. Knowing she recently hadn't been feeling great, on top of the expense of downtown parking and food and drink for four, I had said, "Well, it's probably for the best." Understatement of the century, right?

After picking up Mom at our old house in Dracut, Gia drove like Mario Andretti for the city. Thankfully, I-93 southbound was all but deserted, and every single police officer and state trooper in about a hundred-mile radius was in downtown Boston, not patrolling the highway for speeding cars. As they drove, they listened to WBZ News radio repeat the story over and over, each time adding another tidbit of information, updating the number of injured, and then confirming that three were dead. As they listened, Mom and Gia tried to talk each other, and themselves, down from the rising panic they felt pounding through their chests. On the phone, Gia had told Mom that I was hurt and that my leg might be broken. *Okay, okay, that's not so bad*, Mom had reasoned, but as they listened to the radio, the report getting worse and worse, Gia told her the rest.

"I want you to be prepared, Cookie," Gia said, unconsciously using her daughters' affectionate nickname for their grandmother. Mom, totally lacking the grandmother gene as well as the maternal one, had insisted that the girls not call her "Grandma." She hated the thought of it. So instead they called her Cookie because, rather than feeding the girls healthy snacks like fruit, she'd give them cookies. No matter how loudly or often Gia reprimanded her, Mom would shrug and say, "It works. They stop crying every time." So "Cookie" she became.

"Prepared for what?" Mom asked Gia. "People break their legs all the time."

"Ro's friend said something about a tourniquet. If her leg needs a tourniquet, it could be worse than just broken. I just want you to be ready for bad news."

Mom sat back, lit a cigarette, and silently began to pray.

After reaching the city, they parked the car in a garage and then half walked, half jogged nearly a mile to Mass General. As they neared the hospital, they saw police patrols on every corner and people milling about as if they were at a citywide street party. No one seemed alarmed or panicky or even very upset, just a bit more somber than usual. Just walking, even strolling, some sipping Starbucks, others holding hands and window shopping. Seeing the heavy police presence, Mom suddenly lost it.

"Oh, yeah, this place is lousy with cops *now*. But where the *fuck* were the cops when my daughter got blown up? Tell me that!"

"Come on, Mom, keep moving." But she didn't need to nudge Mom forward; even at close to seventy years old and most of them spent smoking two-plus packs a day, Rose was all but sprinting across the city to her daughter. A fully loaded freight train couldn't have stopped her.

They came through the Mass General doors like storming paratroopers on a mission, panting from the exertion and adrenaline. With their frantic urgency to find me coming off them like sonic waves, hospital and security staff quickly corralled them into a large gray waiting room where dozens of other anxious and terrified family members were gathered.

The first person Rose saw was a priest in full garb, "the white collar and everything," she said later, retelling the story for what felt like the hundredth time. "When I was growing up in Dorchester, you only saw a priest in his black robes when somebody died. I swear to God, I thought he was the angel of death come to tell me you were dead, and I put my hand up and said, 'Get the hell away from me! I don't want to talk to you!'" When he walked away, red-faced and sheepish at having caused such obvious distress, Mom's only thought was *Thank God. He wouldn't walk away if Roseann was dead. He would have had to tell me. Thank. God.*

After her outburst, my very Catholic mother was slightly chagrined at having yelled at a priest, so she allowed herself to be led to the front row of chairs to wait. But that didn't mean she was happy about it. Time and again, she went to a desk at the front of the room, where two elderly women had been assigned to give information to the waiting family members.

"I need to know where my daughter is."

Patient but clearly weary of such queries, one of the women took a deep breath and let it out slowly.

"Yes, ma'am, we know you do. Everybody here wants information on their loved one. But you'll have to return to your seat until we have information on your daughter."

Nope.

"I've waited and waited," Mom said, her voice rising with every word until it was bordering on a scream, "AND I'M NOT WAITING ANYMORE! I WANT TO SEE MY DAUGHTER!"

The women behind the desk leaped to their feet, worried and anxious that the scene was escalating out of their control. Luckily, just then a nurse appeared and headed straight for Mom and Gia.

Patty Harris, RN, was all too familiar with trauma and catastrophic injuries after years of working in Mass General's operating room. Her shift that day had begun as scheduled at 2:30 p.m. Thirty minutes later, she and the doctors and other nurses around her had been told to prepare for mass casualties in the OR. Soon, and for the next ninety minutes, she was immersed in her work, thinking of little beyond the patient in front of her on the gurney. Finally, as the critically injured coming through the OR doors slowed, then stopped, she pulled her phone out of her pocket and saw a text that stopped her cold: "Roseann was hurt and is headed to Mass General. See if you can find her mother and sister downstairs."

Patty quickly ran up to the ICU, determined that I was out of surgery and stable, and took the elevator down to where she knew people were waiting for word about their loved ones. As she entered the room, she saw Mom and Gia by the front desk and approached them. "I'm a friend of Roseann's. She's out of surgery, and she's stable. She's not entirely out of the woods, but it looks like she's going to be okay." Knowing it wasn't her place to tell them the news, Patty didn't say that I had lost my leg below the knee. But Mom wasn't standing for half information.

"Did they amputate her foot?" Mom was still thinking just my foot had been hurt, not my leg from the knee down.

Damn, thought Patty. No getting around this lady—she was not going to wait for the surgeon to give her the news about her daughter. She wanted it then and there, no matter who was delivering it.

"Yes," Patty told her, "they had to take her leg below the knee."

Over the years, Patty had had to deliver her fair share of bad, even devastating news to waiting families, but she had rarely delivered news as grievous as this and watched a mother methodically, even calmly, process the information.

"It was something," Patty told me later, "to watch your mom come to terms with the fact that you had lost a leg but that the bottom line was you were alive. And that's all that mattered. No 'Oh my God!' hysterics. Just 'Thank God she's alive. We can deal with the rest.'"

"Come on," Patty told Mom, gently taking her arm, "let me take you up to see Roseann and her doctor. He can answer all your questions."

Once in the ICU with me, there wasn't much to see. I was out cold, but Dr. King came in and warned Mom and Gia, as well as Dad and Auntie Paula, who had arrived seconds before, that the next twenty-four hours would determine whether I lived or died. Would my body survive the mass trauma it had suffered, or would it go into irreversible shock and multisystem organ failure? Had my lungs suffered invisible but largely fatal blast damage, detectable only once the millions of tiny capillaries in the lungs start filling with blood? The four of them stood by the bed as King delivered the news. Even though he was telling them it was fifty-fifty whether I would live or die, Gia was in such shock that it didn't really sink in. Dad stood by, absorbing the news. Mom, not always the best example of calm under pressure, did what she usually does: she yelled.

"And who gave the authority to amputate her leg?" Mom demanded, her eyes blazing and her anger coming off her like sparks.

King looked at her squarely and said, "There was no authority. I took it off. I had no choice."

Mom wasn't through. "Oh, yeah? And who the hell is going to tell her she doesn't have a leg when she wakes up?"

Again, King's eyes didn't move from hers. "I am."

And with that, Mom was sold on Dr. King. She did, however, ask to see the "before" picture of my leg prior to his amputation, just to put her mind at rest that it might somehow have been possible to save it. When King showed her the photo, she wiped a rare tear from her eye, nodded, and handed the picture back, never again doubting his decision.

After being told there was nothing they could do until I woke up and that they would need all the rest they could get while they could get it, Mom, Dad, and Gia were finally convinced to leave the hospital. When Mom finally got back to her house in Dracut sometime after 10:00 p.m., she found a note stuck in the door. It was from a neighbor and friend whose brother had piloted one of the planes that terrorists had flown into the World Trade Center. Terrorism had hit Dracut close to home, again.

Mom let herself into the house, sat down on the couch, and read the note. It was brief: "I know what you're going through."

Mom put down the note and finally allowed herself to cry.

••••••

I came in and out of a sleep so deep and heavy that I felt like I was lying under a lead blanket, the kind the dental hygienist drapes over you for X-rays—only it felt like I was under about ten of them. While friends and family and nurses and a host of doctors all bustled around me, I was in a semi–dream state, wondering what the hell was going on. When my girlfriends started to filter in, I asked one of them if she thought I'd still be able to go to Cancún that weekend to celebrate our friend Carla's fortieth birthday. I didn't want to miss out on a good time, but I also had no idea of the severity of what had happened. I'd sort of forgotten the little detail about my missing right leg.

Between the drugs and the haze, in a weird and detached way I was actually enjoying the spectacle of it all. Again, I felt like Dorothy in *The Wizard of Oz* after she's been knocked out during the hurricane and is dreaming and watching all the characters of her life whirl by the bedroom window. I recognized most of the faces but wondered why they were milling around. And why, in God's name, was Johnny Abbott, my friend from second grade, hanging around? Was I *that* hurt?

I looked up at him from my hospital bed.

"Johnny," I muttered, fumbling to speak around my thick tongue and reaching up to touch the burned mess I used to call hair, "I'm glad you're here. Everyone's been telling me I look good, but I think they're lying. What do you think? Do I look good?"

"You look like shit," one of my oldest friends in the world said without hesitation. But he wasn't finished with the tough love. "Between the mascara running down your cheeks and that hair, you look like Tammy Faye Bakker and Don King's kid."

Then he sat down on the edge of the bed and did something I had never seen in our forty-year friendship: he cried. It's a good thing Mom wasn't in the room because she would have pinched him and told him not to cry, saying it would only give him puffy eyes and a headache.

······

Before Dr. King brought me out of sedation Tuesday evening, he performed a second surgery to further clean the wound and make sure no hidden shrapnel or other foreign body lingered, either of which would quickly bring about a potentially worse result: infection. Also, he wanted to assess whether he could save enough of the bones in my lower leg for me to end up what they call a BKA: below-the-knee amputee. There is a universe of difference in the rehab process as well as the lifelong savings of an exponentially less expensive prosthesis. Wednesday morning, he brought me the bad news himself: I was scheduled that afternoon for a third and final surgery to remove my leg to about a third of the way up my thigh.

With the morphine flowing through my veins and my awareness of what he was actually telling me not exactly crystal clear, I had a suggestion for the good doctor: "Well, do what you have to do, but can you at least try to make the stump pretty, like a rosebud or something?"

King didn't know quite how to answer that. In all of his thousands of amputations in at least four countries and on three continents, he had never before received such a request. I think I saw him blush, but I can't be sure.

Wednesday afternoon, he removed my knee and about six inches of my femur and closed the stump for good.

······

That Thursday, three days after the bombings, President Barack Obama came to Boston to lead a prayer service for the victims, their families, and really the entire city at Trinity Church in Copley Square, only feet away from the finish line. After the service, he and Michelle Obama visited many of us in the various hospitals around the city who of course couldn't attend. Still dazed and drugged, I was fighting nausea and struggling to focus even on the littlest things. We knew Obama was coming to Mass General, and I tried to make myself a little more presentable, particularly my hair. I turned to Brad, a friend and Boston police officer I had known for years, who was standing by the bed. I looked up and asked if I should cover my stiff, burned hair with the SWAT baseball cap he had brought me from his station. Holding up the cap, I asked, "Cap or no cap?"

Immediately, his answer came back: "Cap. Definitely wear the cap."

Looking down at my hands, already blistered from the burns and with black filth under the nails, I said to Mom, "Can I get a manicure before Obama gets here?"

Mom, in a rare moment of tact, didn't say what she was thinking: *Are you kidding me? Why are you worried about your nails? You should see what the rest of you looks like!*

When President Obama finally came into the room, it was as if he materialized from thin air. One moment there were several dark-suited Secret Service agents rushing about, talking into

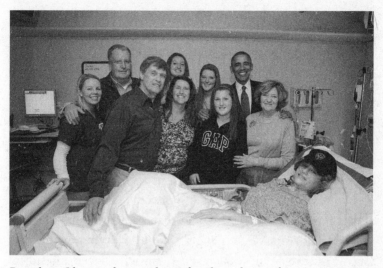

*President Obama along with my family and one of my nurses at my
bedside the Thursday after the bombing.*

Official White House Photo by Pete Souza

their lapels, and the next, *poof*, there he was. What I remember
most about the visit was that he had beautiful skin, and he was
very deferential to Mom. That in itself is surprising, given that
she did nothing but issue demands to him, the president of the
United States.

"Listen," she began, again reaching for her phantom cigarette, "I don't think Roseann or any of these victims should ever
have to pay taxes again."

The president smiled.

"And I want their medical bills covered, 100 percent. None
of these folks should worry about paying their bills."

The president nodded.

"And," she wasn't done, "I want them all on the field to throw
out the first pitch at the Red Sox game."

Finally, Obama couldn't resist. "Well, you know, I'm a White Sox fan. But I'll see what I can do."

Even his Secret Service team cracked up at that one.

Although he couldn't promise a lifetime of tax-free medical care, he did pledge to do everything within his and the country's power to take care of us and to bring those responsible to justice. Before he left, he shook the hand of each person in the room, including my dad, who in contrast to Mom was polite and respectful and encouraged him not to give up the fight for gun reform. President Obama also greeted each of my nieces, all of them tall for their age, and then turned to Gia and Patrick and said, "You've got tall girls like I do." When he hugged Gia, whose eyes were swollen slits from lack of sleep and stolen tears when Mom wasn't looking, her exhausted brain focused on three things: *He's much skinnier than he appears in pictures*, *The collar of his shirt is stiff enough to cut steak*, and *For God's sake, Gia, don't cry on his nice suit!*

She didn't.

······

Later that day, Mom was puttering around my room, chattering on about this and that when she started trying to sell me, it seemed, on the virtues of Mike Materia, the firefighter who had brought me in and who, for all intents and purposes, hadn't yet left.

"Roseann, he is adorable, and so nice."

After he and Pat Foley had been dropped back downtown by the paddy wagon, Mike had instantly sought out two of the other firefighters who had been part of my triage on Boylston and getting me into the paddy wagon, Mike Kennedy and Tommy Cherry, asking them if they knew my name.

"Her first name was Roseann, I remember that," Tommy said.

"She had a weird last name, definitely weird. Starts with an S, I think," Mike Kennedy added.

When Mike's shift finally ended the next morning, he immediately went to Mass General to find me, his arms full of Engine 33/Ladder 15 T-shirts and baseball caps to give to my family. Feeling a sad helplessness that he couldn't do more, he figured he would at least bring some souvenir gifts from the firehouse and see if my family needed anything.

The bombing patients had been admitted under pseudonyms to protect us from possible additional attack. (Mine was "X Brown." While other survivors had great aliases like "Porsche" and "Mercedes" and "Ferrari," I got stuck with "X Brown." No one could ever explain why.) This made it harder to find me, but Mike eventually managed to locate me and learn that I had made it out of surgery. Satisfied that I was alive and out of immediate danger, he and a buddy from Engine 33, Eric Wirtz, who had also been on Boylston Street and helped survivors, headed to the Chantey bar in Quincy's Marina Bay to properly "de-stress."

The next day, Mike was back at Mass General to check on me. Mom says that as soon as she saw Mike in the waiting room, she knew he was special. When he entered the room, Mom relaxed for the first time since before Gia's phone call days earlier.

Mike Materia *was* a curiosity. I started hearing from Mom, Gia, my girlfriends, and even my nieces that he was in the waiting room, seeing if there was anything he could do to help, talking with folks, even bringing coffees and snacks and offering to run errands. Everyone knew he was the firefighter who'd brought me in, and everyone was impressed that he was still there, doing whatever he could to be a steady presence in the middle of such suffering and stress. He later told me that usually when something horrible happened in Boston, a bad car wreck or industrial accident, or even in Iraq, you dealt with it and moved on. You never had to relive the scene or see its victims. But here, it was everywhere—the news, magazines, newspapers. He couldn't even go to the grocery store without that little boy's face looking back at him. In the military, there was something you could do in response to an event: change your SOP (standard operating procedure), research a different strategy, practice, and learn a better way to operate next time. Here, there was no next time. So he carried a heavy gloom around with him, one that lightened every time he walked into the hospital, hoping he could offer help to me and my family.

Mom didn't care why he was there, just that he was. In her mind, she had already married us off and named our children. "He is so cute, and he obviously cares about you," Mom said, sneaking a peek at him standing by the door. You have to hear my mother in person to get the full flavor. I have a Boston accent, but my mother's is straight out of *Good Will Hunting*—thick, strong, and, to the uninitiated ear, almost a foreign language.

"Are you kidding me? I just got blown up, and you're trying to fix me up?" I mumbled, trying to focus on her face but only succeeding in having her voice come through loud and clear.

"Really, Roseann, why would he spend so much time here if he didn't like you?"

She made it sound like we were in fifth grade, not both survivors of a horrible tragedy. And while I also wondered why, in all honesty, I didn't care. I just liked seeing him there.

Mom wasn't the only one singing his praises. A core group of my friends, about six of them, hovered around the waiting room, waiting for me to come out of sedation. After meeting Mike in the waiting room, they rushed to my room, practically tripping over themselves to get through the door and open their computers. They immediately did what savvy single girls do in that circumstance: they Googled him and found his Facebook page.

"Ohhh, he's so *cute!*" one gushed.

"Oh, my God, he's at the Boylston Street firehouse. That's so cool," another said.

"No creepy photos or weird posts, either. Plus, doesn't say anything here about a girlfriend," another added.

Through their planning of my big, fat Boston wedding, I tried to remember details of his getting me off the street, into the van, and into the ER. But only one thing came sharply into focus: I remembered banging on the poor man's chest, insisting he hold my hand. And he had. That much I remembered clearly.

One day, as Mom and some of my girlfriends quizzed Mike about his job, his family, and, yes, if he was dating anyone, Mike quietly blushed all the way to the top of his shaved head. Out of nowhere, I turned to him and burst out, "You are way too young for me to date, you know!"

Mike smiled and quietly said, "I don't remember asking."

For the first time since the blast, I laughed. He may have been too young for me, but he was quick and, yes, he was cute.

After he left that day, Gia called his cell phone and left a message.

"Please come back," Gia said, her voice breaking. "Today was the first time I've seen her smile or laugh since it happened. Please. Come back."

Mike listened to my sister's tearful message twice, each time feeling something kick against his chest wall, kind of like that little fist he remembered from the paddy wagon. Mike texted Gia and told her that he would indeed return.

Officer Shana Cottone also came to my room that Thursday afternoon after Obama's visit. It had taken her a while to find where I was in Mass General, but she remembered my first name and had Googled me. Although the hospitals had us all code-named, our real names were already being posted on the Internet. So much for hospital security. As Shana peeked around the door frame, I could have sworn I saw her square her shoulders, shoring up her strength to come in. She looked as if she were thinking, *No one wants to see a cop cry.* When she finally did come into the room, she was anything but meek. She came right over to the bed and, as she had on Boylston Street, leaned down so that our noses were practically touching.

"We're gonna get those motherfuckers who did this! I promise you, we're going to get them!" she said.

Mom, usually reserved with public displays of affection and downright stingy with hugs, turned to Shana and immediately wrapped her arms around her.

Really? I thought, watching the scene from my bed. *This cop throws a couple of "motherfuckers" around the room and gets a hug, and I lose a leg and so far the most I've gotten from her is a pat on the arm.* I wish I had had the strength to say it out loud. Everyone would have laughed.

"Isn't she sweet?" Mom gushed to the others in the room.

Sweet? Seriously?

But as I thought about Shana's words, I realized that it hadn't occurred to me until that moment that there were any "motherfuckers" to get. I had truly had no idea. I had kept my eyes clamped shut against the horror around me on Boylston Street—most of it, at least—and was blissfully unaware of the true scope of the attack. In the days that followed, my mind had struggled to make sense of the chaos in a textbook attempt to regain some control after being so utterly powerless. And I think my Italian Catholic guilt kept bringing back to me the idea that *I* must have done something wrong. But with Shana's outburst, I began to wonder whether what had happened might be a lot bigger than simply a personal attack aimed at me.

While I came in and out of consciousness, recovering from and then gearing up for yet another surgery, fighting the pain and then the nausea caused by the painkillers, and just trying to clear the fog from my brain, I had no idea a massive manhunt had shut down the city. By Thursday, police had identified the two bombers, Tamerlan and Dzhokhar Tsarnaev, young brothers who had been born in Chechnya but had emigrated to America as boys. Before it was all over, they would claim yet another life: Sean Collier, a twenty-six-year-old MIT police officer whom they ambushed while he sat in his patrol car. Three days after the bombing, a violent shootout in nearby Watertown left one of the brothers dead and the other on the run. Not knowing how many more bombs and weapons might be in his possession, Massachusetts governor Deval Patrick called for an emergency "shelter in place," which emptied the streets of Boston while police went door to door searching for the second brother. Fifteen hours later, they found him, alive and hiding in a dry-docked boat in a quiet Watertown neighborhood west of Boston.

When it was over, and the "motherfuckers" were either dead or captured, the city rejoiced. People from Watertown to Boston came out of their houses, poured into the streets, and celebrated as only Bostonians can do. Police and firefighters became instant heroes, were bought coffee and food, and were treated like the heroes they were. As they pulled out of the neighborhoods, their caravans of cruisers, ambulances, fire trucks, SWAT armored vehicles, and paddy wagons became a parade through the streets, with thousands of citizens screaming their thanks. We were safe. We had our city back. The nightmare was over.

But for me, in many ways it was just beginning.

chapter seven

THE KID WITH THE TOURNIQUET

A WEEK AFTER the bombing, and finally out of the woods medically, I was transferred to the Spaulding Rehabilitation Center with several other critically wounded survivors of the blast. Eventually, thirty-one survivors and fourteen of the seventeen who had lost limbs ended up in Spaulding. We called it the "old Spaulding"—a grim, dingy building from the 1970s. It sat, sad and ugly, on a spit of land amid the North Station train tracks and across the street from the Nashua Street jail. But at least it wasn't Mass General. It had a lot of the same antiseptic sights and smells, but it was a place for healing, not merely surviving, and I was more than ready to heal.

Most times when I woke up, Mom or Dad or Gia or one of my girlfriends would be sitting nearby, lightly dozing or reading a book. I can't remember a time when I was alone in the room. They'd notice I was awake, and more often than not, they'd tell me that the firefighter, Mike Materia, was in the waiting room, just, well, waiting. For what I didn't know. But just knowing he was close by and seeing him there in my room, shy and always in the background, almost as if standing guard, gave me what little comfort I had in the weeks following the attack. After Gia's call to him asking him to come back, he did—almost every day.

······

From almost the first moment after Dr. King had brought me out of my induced coma, images of a young man—a kid, really—had filtered through my hazy memory of the attack, arms firmly around my body, being carried, hands pulling hard on a belt—no, a *tourniquet*.

"Dad?" I said, looking over at him in the chair next to my bed.

He was exhausted. The wear and worry of the past week were etched deeply into his face. He had been to see me just about every day since the bombing, even though his girlfriend, Lennie, and his mother were also dealing with serious health issues. (My grandmother would succumb to her terminal cancer within the year.) He jumped up and was instantly alert by my bed.

"What? Are you okay? Do you need anything?"

"There was someone who picked me up off the sidewalk and carried me to safety in the middle of the street. Does anyone know who he is? He came out of nowhere, just appeared through the smoke. He was my guardian angel."

Dad smiled and nodded. "Yup. He saved your life as much as anybody did. But nobody knows who he is."

"Let's find him, okay?"

······

Shores Salter always considered himself a very lucky guy. And by any measure, he was. Even a cursory glance through the

Salter family photo album shows one picture after another of healthy, handsome, upper-middle-class folks having a hell of a good time: playing tennis, boating around Cape Cod Bay on a cabin cruiser, sailing through the British Virgin Islands, playing Twister on a pristine beach, gathered over lobster dinners in seafront restaurants, all lined up, one more good-looking than the next, smiling in their Christmas sweaters by the tree. It's actually hard not to be a little jealous. While, on many different levels, my, Mike's, and Shana's childhoods can all be described as unsettled at times, Shores's childhood in bucolic Reading, Massachusetts, makes the *Leave It to Beaver* family look dysfunctional. His parents, Bob and Lorraine, fell in love when they were still teenagers and remain devoted to each other. Shores and his two older brothers, Ian and Cam, were raised with love (sometimes tough love), and as if that isn't enough already, each of them has natural athletic ability and Hollywood good looks.

Even after having two older boys, Lorraine knew Shores was going to be her biggest challenge. Just before his birth, she sat transfixed, feeling the baby inside her belly do somersaults and watching his tiny feet pushing off against her huge belly for another spin. A few days later, when labor started, the doctor told her that the baby was breech and proceeded to flip Shores around so that he was head-, not feet-, first. But as soon as he was turned, Shores flipped right back into breech position, almost as if unwilling to leave his warm, comfy nest inside his mother. After several failed attempts to turn and keep the baby in the anterior position, Lorraine reluctantly agreed to a C-section to get Shores safely out into the world. Two weeks later, just as she and Bob were settling into life with their third son and new baby in the house, Shores developed pyloric stenosis, a rare disorder of the lower stomach, which is a tricky condition to diagnose. Thankfully, the doctors quickly recognized it as PS and treated him before he became critically ill. It would be just about his last physical ailment. But that's not to say he didn't spend a lot of time in doctors' offices, mostly orthopedic doctors, for a near-constant stream of broken arms and wrists, dislocated knees and fingers, the occasional mild concussion and missing tooth. Shores was a dangerous combination of adventurous and injury-prone.

••••••

Always a gregarious kid, as a toddler Shores would sidle up to the prettiest woman in the room, hop into her lap, and reach up to twirl her hair, smiling the whole time. Everywhere he went, adults gravitated to the chubby, charming "Buddha Baby," as his godmother nicknamed him. Everyone always wanted to pick him up. He would immediately cuddle into their laps and, if it was a woman, reach up and absentmindedly play with her hair. By the time he was four, Shores was known to practically everyone in town, from the cashiers at the grocery store to the gas-station attendants to the kids selling ice cream at the Dandilyons' drive-through window.

"Hey! Shores!" they'd call out with a smile and a wave.

"Who's that?" Lorraine would ask, never having met the person.

While Shores couldn't remember all of their names, they all remembered *his* because of his easy smile and open arms to the world around him. Lorraine and Bob called him the Mayor.

••••••

Shores seemed to be born with a sense of concern, even worry, for those around him, particularly his mother. When Lorraine was alone in the living room playing the piano, three-year-old Shores would plunk himself next to her on the bench and insist, "Poor Mommy, you need someone with you." To this day, his concern for her makes Lorraine a little teary. When he was four, he found her bent over the piano keys, concentrating hard on the piece she was playing, and asked, "Are you crying, Mama, 'cuz it looked like you was." He was also fixated on her dying, or rather, her *not* dying. One morning, she awoke to find his face staring at her over the edge of the bed. "See, Mommy? You didn't die, you was just sleepin'."

Shores's mother earned her degree in speech pathology from Emerson College, with which she hoped to move to New York and work with actors on dialects and accents. But after graduation and by then married, she found herself in suburban Boston rather than some artsy neighborhood of SoHo, so she started her own speech therapy practice, working out of her living room. By the time Shores came along, ten years and two sons later, her clientele consisted largely of children with special needs—autism, mild retardation, and severe speech impediments. Coming home from school, Shores would stop by the living room to greet his mother as well as whatever kid was sitting on the couch getting their therapy.

"Hey, buddy!" Shores greeted Kevin, a boy three years younger than he with severe autism.

Kevin's perpetually dour face lit up like a neon sign, his rare smile coming easily and openly to Shores.

"Wassup, dude!" Shores said, fist-bumping Kevin, before giving his mother a quick kiss on the cheek and heading into the kitchen for a snack.

Over the years, Shores greeted scores of children in his living room, each as if they were friends, never shunning them for their oddity or patronizing their disability. Shores hated to see kids bullied or shunned, as the oddballs and outcasts often were at the tony country clubs where he played tennis and the even tonier summer community of Chatham on Cape Cod.

As much as he was a good kid who watched out for those around him, he was also what both of his parents called a "knucklehead," prone to mischief and the kid who took the rap when the other, older boys got them into trouble. Shores grew up surrounded by brothers, cousins, and his best friend, Charlie, all of whom were never far from his daily life. But, being the youngest kid at most of the gatherings, Shores was the one every older boy loved to beat on. Watching her son on the trampoline from the kitchen window, Lorraine would wonder at how he would take his licks from the older kids, get whacked, swatted, and pushed off the trampoline onto his head, over and over, and never complain, never come running to Mama, never tattle on his abusers. He'd just climb back up on the trampoline and start jumping again, the happiest kid on the block. He also had a preternatural calm about taking other kids' ribbing. When he was about ten, he got a huge wad of resin in his hair while helping repair his father's surfboard. Unable to get the hardened glue out, Bob gave Shores a buzz cut, which only exaggerated his already large head. Of course, his new nickname became Melon Head, soon shortened to Melon, and then just Mel. Soon after, when he and Charlie (also sporting a buzz cut for the summer) signed in to their summer camp, the counselors instantly dubbed them Mel and Chuck. Shores wore the moniker with pride.

As he grew, he and Charlie became more like brothers than just best friends. Not only did they attend every day of school together, most years in the same class, but they were equally popular. Each year they would run for and get elected as class president and vice president, respectively; then the next year they would trade off and run for and win in opposite seats. Charlie says they weren't popular in the way that jocks are but that they had friends from every group and clique, from the smart kids to the special needs kids. So at election time, they tapped into that broad fan base.

•••••

Shores and Charlie also had a golden touch at organizing. Whether it was operating "the Saltiner Store," a mobile kiosk named by combining Salter and Kaminer, Charlie's last name, selling sodas and chips out of a wagon they pulled around tennis tournaments, or starting "Super Fans," a loose collection of friends who would gather and cheer at the games they didn't play in, they were universally liked, even admired, by nearly all of their classmates and teachers. Perhaps because of Lorraine's work with children with disabilities, perhaps because of his own rock-solid sense of himself, Shores was always at ease with developmentally and physically challenged kids. He believed the only way for everyone to get more comfortable with each other was through exposure, so he was part of bringing the challenged and the "typically developing" kids together in the same social gatherings—school dances, sports events, even tennis matches.

That's not to say that Shores didn't screw up, like the times he and Charlie would shoot hockey pucks at his garage windows for target practice. Or the times they would wake up laughing, recounting the previous night's adventures after having had several beers too many. He was also infamous for putting his proverbial foot in his mouth. Early on in college, a buddy who bartended at Daisy Buchanan's on Newbury Street would text Shores and other close friends whenever a sports celebrity came into the restaurant. One night Shores got word that his favorite Bruins player was there and rushed down to meet him. When he saw the man sitting at the bar talking to a woman— a woman who didn't seem to be as engrossed in the conversation as Shores thought she should be—Shores couldn't resist approaching when the woman walked away from the bar.

"Dude," offered Shores, "you could have any lady in here you want. I wouldn't worry about *that* lady."

The Bruin gave Shores a withering look. "*Dude*, that *lady* is my sister!"

Shores retreated before the man could land any blows.

Like many Boston-area college students, Shores, by this time a Northeastern University "middler" in his third year, wasn't running the marathon; he was cruising various bars along Boylston Street with a small posse of buddies. After a few hours at Dillon's, a bar at the top of Boylston Street right next to the Engine 33/Ladder 15 firehouse, he and a friend from Tufts University decided to head toward Daisy Buchanan's. They started down Boylston, sometimes moving faster than the runners who'd been at it for over four hours, and passed in front of the Prudential Center, Boston's first and most recognizable skyscraper. It was 2:49 p.m. when they felt and heard, rather than saw, an explosion of some sort farther down the street. Nearer the finish, from the sound of it.

"What the? . . ." Shores asked no one in particular, the words floating unnoticed in the air while he and everyone around him tried to make sense of what had just happened. It was odd timing for a cannon, too loud for a manhole cover, too strong for a transformer. *Then what the* . . . But no sooner had his brain registered the shock than, just across the street, a second explosion shook the ground beneath his feet, the blast so close he could feel the violent change in air pressure against his face.

He reflexively flinched, shutting his eyes against the blast. When he opened them, it was to mayhem. Amid the acrid smoke, men, women, and children were screaming, and people were running in all directions, not knowing where the blast had originated. The dense smoke filled the air with a cloying smell he didn't recognize but later learned was burned flesh.

"We gotta get the fuck out of here," his buddy yelled over the clamor.

Shores nodded and followed his friend, who began sprinting down Boylston. In their confusion and the screaming panic around him, Shores was unaware that he was heading straight into the chaos of the first blast.

Suddenly, Shores stopped. His buddy kept running and disappeared into the panic and smoke.

Why am I running? Shores thought. *There are people back there who are hurt. I saw the bodies. I saw the body parts. I saw the blood. Why am I running away?*

When the World Trade Center towers were hit on September 11, 2001, Shores was not yet nine. While he was too young to comprehend the specifics at the time, the boy remembered the lingering and pervasive terror after the attack. But eleven years later, two separate shootings would change his notion of "innocent bystander" forever. On July 20, 2012, a lone gunman walked into a movie theater in Aurora, Colorado, and opened fire, killing twelve and injuring seventy more. Five months after that, another lone gunman calmly walked through an elementary school in Newtown, Connecticut, killing twenty children and six teachers. Watching coverage of these massacres, Shores's overriding thought was *If I ever am in that kind of situation, I hope to God I do something—tackle the gunman, protect others by lying on top of them, whatever I have to do.*

That moment came only a few months later.

After the second bomb went off on Boylston Street, Shores started to run but then stopped. He turned around and tried to clear his head. He had sobered up fast before, but never this fast. Still dazed but focused, he stood in the lingering smoke and rising stench, trying to figure out what to do. Then, without wasting any more time getting his bearings or rationalizing the best course of action, he ran into the smoke and toward the bloodbath where bodies and body parts lay scattered on the ground. Amid the screams and chaos, a voice rang out clearly—mine.

"Help me, please! Can anyone help me?"

Turning toward the voice, he saw me on the ground, my left hand still holding my ringing ears. Focusing on my face and not the ruined mess underneath me, he bent down.

"Are you all right?" he asked.

I shook my head. He moved to help me get up.

"Come on, you need to get off the sidewalk."

Amid all the madness that was to come, all the shouting, screaming, and wild butchery of the day, Shores told me that the words I said next forever etched themselves into his memory.

"I can't," I cried. "I don't have my leg."

Shores felt something hard and solid hit the bottom of his stomach: dread. While he didn't closely examine my wounds, he could see that I was losing a lot of blood and that my right leg was pinned underneath me.

"Yes, your leg is still there, I promise. But we have to get you off the sidewalk." He hadn't seen where the first bomb had detonated, but he had been close enough to the second to feel the blast and knew that it had been on the sidewalk.

Something about his tenderness, his youthful urgency, acted like a chisel to my stoic resolve, and I felt my eyes well up. *Someone is helping me; maybe I won't die right here on the curb.*

"Come on, I'll carry you. Hold on to me. We gotta get you out of here."

He reached down to grasp under my arms and hoist me up, rag-doll style.

Although it seemed to him as if it had happened over the course of several hours, Shores would later learn that in less than a minute, the second bomb had gone off, he had started running, turned around, run back, found me, and carried me away from the curb. Less than a minute. And even though to this day he doesn't like to talk about what happened next, it is nothing short of miraculous. He saved my life. It is that simple. While scores of people ran away and others ghoulishly took pictures and videos on their cell phones, Shores did what no one else did: he heard my calls for help and came to me, a hideously wounded stranger sitting in the middle of those already dead and dying.

He pulled me up, and we did our weird stumble dance across Boylston Street, but Shores had no idea where he was taking me. If my dangling right foot hadn't been flapping around and making me woozy to the point of nearly vomiting, God only knows where we would have ended up.

"Please, put me down," I told him.

Just as he started to, two men approached us.

Nick Robertson and Matt Fulchino had been watching the race in front of the Lord & Taylor department store, less than a hundred feet away, when the second bomb exploded. Knowing that they had just witnessed explosions, and both having medical training, Matt and Nick pushed the police barricades down to get to the other side of the street, the side with the bombs and the injured.

After an initial eerie calm, silence even, after the second bomb, the street became crowded with screaming and panicky people trying to get away: it looked like the running of the bulls, only in the middle of a battlefield.

Like Shores before him, Matt thought, *We aren't running away.* He turned to Nick and said, "We are going to help these people."

As they looked around them, trying to determine where they were needed most, they saw a tall young man coming toward them carrying a woman whose lower right leg was a mangled mess of flesh and broken, exposed bones.

"Put her down here, man," Nick told Shores, who laid me down as gently as he could.

Matt, an engineer and also a trained EMT, went through the ABC checklist on me: Airway, okay. Breathing, okay. Circulation—stable, but it probably wouldn't be for long.

I was critical, but amazingly, my leg was not gushing blood at that point. When you look at my path from the mailbox to where they laid me on Boylston Street, there is no blood trail. Later Matt would explain that in traumatic amputations, the body immediately employs a list of lifesaving devices—among the first being that the severed artery in effect "curls" back on itself as well as often self-cauterizing, both of which slow the flow of blood. Finally, as Dr. King later explained, the blood pressure crashes so that less blood is being pumped through the heart in the first place. But, at some point—and when that point comes differs from body to body and depends on yet another list of factors—all hell was going to break loose, and with it the remaining blood in my body. All that Nick and Matt knew was that at some point, soon, my curled or cauterized artery and low blood pressure wouldn't be enough to prevent a renewed arterial bleed, and they would need something to save my life: a tourniquet.

"She needs a tourniquet," Matt said. "Here, use my belt." He quickly tore it from his waist and, because he was closer to my head while Nick was at my leg, handed the belt to Nick.

Nick picked up my leg, threaded the belt underneath it, looped the end through the buckle, and pulled it tight.

Suddenly, a Boston cop appeared and ordered, "Okay, clear out of here! If you're not a medical professional, get the fuck out of here. We need to clear the area!"

Suddenly, another bystander appeared, kneeling near my head. "I'm a doctor. You guys had better clear out," he said to Nick and Matt.

Nick nodded. "You got this?" he asked Shores.

In the chaos of the moment and Nick's laser focus on my leg and nothing else, he assumed he was handing the tourniquet off to the doctor. But when I told him later that the doctor was on the *other* side of my body and that it was Shores who took control of the tourniquet, he was stunned.

"I just assumed it was the doctor who took over," he said. "After all, he was the real medical professional on the scene."

But again, it was Shores who, for the second time that day, took on a burden that was not his to shoulder. He grabbed hold of the belt for dear life. My life.

Knowing that the basic function of a tourniquet was to be tight but trying not cause me any more pain than he had to,

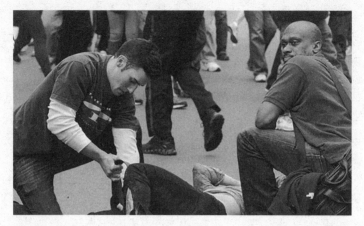

This is the photo that was used to locate Shores. It was taken moments after he laid me down on the street and was given the belt as a makeshift tourniquet. You can see the look of distress on both his and Dr. Collin Stultz's faces.

Courtesy of Bill Hoenk Photography

Shores looked around him, desperate for direction. He felt as if he was asking the air, anyone, everyone, for help.

"Is there such a thing as *too* tight?" he pleaded, looking at the man across from him.

"No," Dr. Collin Stultz said. "You have to pull as hard as you possibly can."

So Shores pulled. I let out a scream, but he didn't release the tension on the belt. He also braced his left hand against my thigh for leverage as he pulled with his right, his hands turning white with the effort. That simple act of pushing his hand against my severed femoral artery and vein and applying direct pressure to the wound did more to keep me on this Earth than any other single thing.

I didn't know it then, but improvised tourniquets, like those made from leather belts, for instance, almost never work. The person holding the tourniquet simply cannot maintain enough continual force to stop the flow of blood through the body's main arteries. The fact that an untrained college kid with a few too many beers in him administered the tourniquet and then held that belt while maintaining direct pressure on the open wound is, to quote Dr. King, "amazing."

Dr. Stultz thought so too. As he monitored my vitals and kept me talking to determine whether my brain was still functioning, he looked down to make sure the bleeding was controlled. It was.

"You're doing a great job," he said to Shores as calmly and forcefully as he could, knowing that panic could be just as deadly to the victims as a bomb. It worked. When Shores finally told me his version of the triage, he kept talking about how Stultz had been his anchor in the storm, letting him know he was doing it right and keeping him focused on the tension on the belt.

Months later, when I finally went through the chain of events, I realized there were nearly a dozen people and first responders who had received some medical training who were buzzing around me, from Nick and Matt to Dr. Stultz, who supervised Shores, to several cops and on- and off-duty firefighters, all of whom were part of the reason I am here today. But it was twenty-year-old Shores Salter who held the belt. Yes, most of them were multitasking while attending to other victims, and many did tell him he had to pull harder, but when it came to it, a kid took the responsibility upon himself and did the job. And I think it was that burden that so haunted him in the weeks to come.

When I was finally loaded into the van and Shores watched it pull away and disappear up Ring Road, his first emotion was regret: *I should have stayed on to help.* He was overcome with anguish: Had he saved me, or had he done me more harm? Why hadn't he stayed in the paddy wagon? Why had he let it drive away, not even knowing my name? What if he never saw me again? What if he never heard whether I had lived or died? When the van disappeared around the corner, he turned back toward the chaos, seeing if there was someone else who needed help.

"We're clearing this area! What the fuck are you still doing here?" demanded a Boston cop.

"I want to help!" Shores said.

"No, get out of here, kid. Stay safe. We're locking the entire area down."

Shores turned away and walked up the same street down which he had seen the paddy wagon disappear. He headed through the backstreets toward his apartment on Tremont Street. His ears were ringing in the momentary lull of sirens. It was almost eerie after the cacophony of Boylston Street.

Thirty miles to the north, Bob Salter was at his desk when a coworker came rushing in. "There was an explosion at the marathon. They're saying it could have been a bomb!"

Bob felt the immediate reflexive jolt of a parent whose child could be in danger. He knew that Shores was probably cruising through the bars and the streets on Marathon Monday. But he prided himself on being a man of reasoned emotions and collected calm in the face of emergency, so his hand was steady as he dialed his son's number and listened to it ring.

"Dad?" Shores picked up on the third ring. He almost wept when he heard his father's voice.

"Shores, are you okay?"

His father's calm helped settle him. Shores took a ragged breath, willing himself to hold it together.

"Yeah. I'm okay."

"What happened down there?"

As he started to tell his father the story, Shores's calm broke and he started weeping. "It was so fucked up, Dad. *Just fucked up*. There was an explosion, and there were body parts all over." Shores looked down at himself. "I have blood all over me, all over my shoes."

But what Shores didn't tell his father, or anyone in any real detail for several weeks, was exactly *what* he had done on the streets of downtown Boston. Instead he spoke of the scene and its ghoulish barbarity. It was nothing even the most seasoned war veterans had been prepared for, let alone a twenty-year-old college kid.

"Shores, listen to me," Bob said, hoping to give Shores something to focus on besides his own rising shock. "Your cousins were at the marathon; do you know if they're okay? I need you to call them and make sure they're okay. Can you do that?"

"Yes," Shores answered, wiping his eyes and nose with the back of his hand. "Yes. I have their numbers."

"Good. But get home first, okay? Get off the street."

"Okay, Dad. I will."

After Shores hung up, he realized he hadn't asked his father to make sure his mother knew he was okay. He punched the button for "Mom" on his phone, but nothing happened— no ring, no busy signal, nothing. He didn't know if his phone was dead or the system was down, so he stopped a woman who had her phone in her hand and asked if he could use it. As she handed it over, she gaped at his pants and shoes: they were red and slick with blood.

"Mom, there was a bomb," Shores started, but his emotion again choked him. It was a few moments before he could continue. "I saw some ridiculous shit down here. It was just crazy; there were bombs, and people's bodies were all over the street."

Like her husband, Lorraine struggled to impart calm to her son, but ambulances and police sirens again swirled around Shores, and they could barely hear each other. A few of them sounded way too close. She tried not to scream over the noise.

"Shores, I need you to make sure you're not in the street," she said, forcing herself to breathe deeply and slowly. *Calm down, Lorraine, calm down.* "Shores? Honey, are you there? I need you to make sure you're off the street. Get on the sidewalk and get home, okay? Call me when you get there, please?"

He told her he would and that he loved her. Then he hung up. He thanked the woman and handed back her phone.

"Are you okay?" she asked.

Shores nodded, unable to speak, and walked away.

He cried all the way to his apartment. He got to his apartment building, realized he didn't have his keys, and hit the buzzer. Almost immediately, his roommate, Angelo, answered the door.

"Dude," Angelo said, taking in the blood and tears and shock on his friend's face. Before he could say or ask anything, Shores stumbled across the threshold, practically into Angelo's arms, and allowed himself to be guided into the apartment.

Shores sat on the couch mute, almost catatonic, his breath coming in ragged gasps. His eyes kept returning to his jeans and once-tan canvas sneakers, now both splattered with blood. Seeing his distress, Angelo silently knelt down and removed Shores's ruined shoes, tucking them out of sight by the front door. It would be hours before Shores spoke and many days before he could tell Angelo what had happened.

For the next several days, Shores remained locked in his own world, sitting transfixed in front of the television, watching the 24-7 news coverage of the bombing, scouring every word and image for news of the victims. Specifically, for news of me. He didn't know my name. In the insanity of those twenty minutes with me and maintaining his superhuman hold on that belt, he hadn't thought to ask. He was haunted by the terrible savagery of it all and the lingering anguish of "what if." *What if I didn't hold the tourniquet correctly? What if I actually hurt the woman versus helped her? What if I could have done more to help her?* And the worst "what if" of all: *What if I never know if she lived or died?* He combed through every report, looking for news of the dead and the wounded. His heart sank when he read that one of those who had died, Krystle Campbell, also had blond hair. But then he learned that Krystle had been at the site of the *first* bomb, not the second. As he pored through reports and articles, he read one that mentioned another victim, Heather Abbott, who had also been at Forum and had lost her *left* foot in the blast. But as Shores replayed the scene in his head over and over, he saw the tourniquet and his hand applying direct pressure on my right leg, not my left. Still, he worried that his memory was faulty, given the chaos and the beers. So he kept trying to identify me and hoping I was still alive.

Not only was he tormented by not knowing whether I had lived or died, but the aftershock of the bombing and the entire nation's collective outrage at once again being hit in the heart in one of their beloved cities weighed heavily on him. The hunt for the culprits had begun only hours after the bombings, and by Thursday afternoon, the FBI had released photos of the Tsarnaev brothers as the prime suspects. They were on the run, hijacking cars and throwing explosive devices at anything in their way. Shortly after midnight on Friday, April 19, the brothers shot and killed MIT police officer Sean Collier as he sat in his cruiser, then fled in a hijacked car. Soon after, the car was spotted in Watertown, just west of Cambridge, where a gun battle ensued and the elder brother, Tamerlan, was killed when Dzhokhar ran over him as he sped away from the scene. By Friday morning, a "shelter in place" lockdown had been issued for a metro area of five million residents while police, the FBI, the ATF, and Homeland Security went door to door searching for the second bomber.

Terrorism had come to the streets of Boston, and Shores was watching every minute of it.

Up in Reading, where life remained somewhat normal, Lorraine and her best friend, Kate, were having lunch when Shores called his mother. Across the table, Kate read Lorraine's face like a book, listening to her tense replies.

"Shores, there's a shelter in place, I can't come get you. . . . I know, I know, but you have to calm down."

She hung up, and the women looked at each other for a moment in silence before Kate waved for the check.

"Okay, let's go," Kate said.

Lorraine didn't argue. Within the hour, the two women were driving through Boston, past police cruisers and SWAT trucks, the only other vehicles on the streets. Lorraine worried that they might be pulled over and stopped.

"What? They're going to stop two middle-aged women in a shit-box Subaru?" Kate said, allowing them both a badly needed laugh.

Their laughter soon died in their throats when they neared the BU Bridge and looked up Commonwealth Avenue. What they saw has probably never before happened on the streets of

Boston and may never again: there wasn't a soul or a car in sight. They marveled that their bustling city had turned into a ghost town. It looked like Armageddon, Kate thought. You could have heard a pin drop in the middle of the six-lane street.

Shores was waiting for them on his front stoop, eager and agitated to get the hell out of the city. Throwing his laundry into the backseat, he climbed in after it and barked at his mother, "Go! Just drive!"

Kate and Lorraine looked at each other as Lorraine put the car in gear. Shores was not a kid to bark orders, but they knew this was no time for a lesson in good manners. He was as jittery as a junkie needing a fix. Kate thought, *The poor kid is practically crawling out of his skin.* His neck veins were popping, and his eyes darted nervously from window to window.

They drove through Boston's famed medical area near the Fenway. Armed guards were stationed with machine guns in front of the Beth Israel Deaconess Medical Center. They didn't know it then, but that was where one of the bombers had been taken after the police shootout and now lay dead in the morgue. The second bomber remained at large.

"Where the hell *is* that other guy?" Shores suddenly exploded from the backseat.

The women jumped. Lorraine, ever the mom, tried to calm her son down with small talk, asking him if he was hungry; did they need to stop and get something to eat?

"NO! Just drive!"

Again, the women gave each other a glance, and Lorraine drove on in silence, both of them thinking, *Jeez, this kid needs help.*

By 9:00 that evening, the second bomber had been found and arrested, and after more than twelve hours of being locked down in their own homes, hundreds of thousands of Boston residents flooded the streets and reclaimed their city.

But in Reading, Shores remained in his own private prison, an uncharacteristic darkness surrounding him. When asked, he told his family simply that he had been there and seen "a lot of bad shit," but he didn't tell them just what he had seen, or that he had been up to his elbows in it.

It would be another two weeks before he would be able to.

chapter eight

LET THE HEALING BEGIN

MEANWHILE, BACK AT the old Spaulding, I was still woozy with pain meds and somewhat foggy, but after my first shower in over a week, I was definitely feeling better and solid enough to start talking to reporters, many of whom had been clamoring for interviews since the bombing. Teary but coherent, I thought my interviews went okay. In one of the first, I told my longtime friend and WCVB-TV reporter, Kathy Curran, that I remembered a guardian angel who had gotten me off the sidewalk and applied the tourniquet that had saved my life. And I wanted to find him.

······

After only a few days at the old Spaulding, we were moved to the rehab center's sparkling new building, which had just opened. As I packed up my room, I decided one thing would definitely stay behind: my wheelchair. For me, a wheelchair symbolized permanency and immobility, and I hated it.

I know that untold thousands of military veterans and accident victims and survivors of devastating diseases need and rely on chairs for their very movement through life. For them, wheelchairs are not only a symbol of freedom, they are independence itself. Those people have my utmost respect: I have the luxury of being able to refuse to use a wheelchair, and they don't.

Even though it meant crutching around on one leg until I got my prosthesis, and I was still weeks away on the recovery scale, the wheelchair was staying. I still had one leg; I was determined to walk again.

Another albatross I was ready to ditch was the IV port in my arm that had been used for my many blood transfusions and gallons of replacement fluids. Throughout my stay in Mass General and then the old Spaulding, the staff had had to move the port whenever one vein failed and another had to be found. I have always hated needles, and after untold needle pricks and port changes, I was more than ready for a new, port-free start. Losing it was an important milestone for me in regaining my health.

An ambulance took me to the new Spaulding. I hate ambulances because being strapped in makes me feel claustrophobic and trapped. But the drive was beautiful. From Boston, we went over the Charlestown Bridge, along the waterfront, past the USS *Constitution* and old Charlestown Navy Yard, and to the end of a spit of land that had been an active navy base for most of the nineteenth and twentieth centuries.

The Spaulding Rehab Center was so new that I and the other marathon patients were its first patients, and we all marveled at our five-star room-with-an-ocean-view luxury after the dreariness of our various hospital and previous rehab rooms. I definitely felt better at the new Spaulding, but I was far from feeling good. In fact, no sooner had I been admitted than I was rushed back to Mass General with kidney failure. So much for being out of the woods.

I did not handle it well. To be honest, I had a meltdown. First of all, I was still processing what had happened to me back on Boylston Street. When I saw other amputees and bombing survivors in their wheelchairs or in physical therapy next to me, I had no idea that some of us shared the experience of having our limbs amputated by a bomb at the marathon. All I knew was that I was getting sick and tired of the endless tests and needles and drugs that come with any trauma surgery. So when the urologist came into my room and told me that I was being transferred *back* to Mass General for emergency dialysis that afternoon, I absolutely lost it, full of panic and confusion.

What were they not telling me? I was discharged in the morning only to be readmitted hours later? Were they really going to release me from the hospital after the dialysis or keep me indefinitely? What else was wrong with me that I didn't know about? What did they mean when they said they were going to insert a catheter— like a urine catheter? No, they told me they were going to cut into the femoral artery in my groin and insert a tube! A tube! What did they mean? WHAT WAS GOING ON?

Every time they tried to say something to make me feel better, it just made it worse. I felt as if I was going backward, not moving forward. It took them two hours and I dare say a fair dose of Valium to get me calm enough to insert the femoral catheter and begin the four-hour process of jump-starting my kidneys back into doing their job of ridding my body and blood of toxins. Even so, throughout the procedure my chest felt heavy with fluid; my old asthma kicked in, making it hard to breathe, and I kept calling the nurse over, asking her to make sure I wasn't dying. I wasn't, but it sure felt like I was at the time.

Along with everything else, the bomb basically screwed up my kidneys. Unbeknownst to me, the doctors had been monitoring their function for days, worried about their ever-weaker performance. As a result, the nurses had been urging me to drink water like a camel in a desert oasis, so much so that it became something of a joke, given what a pain in the butt it was to get to the bathroom. With my small bladder, what had always been an annoyance *before* the bombing became a downright nuisance after it: ringing for the nurse, getting help maneuvering into the wheelchair, getting help into the bathroom, maneuvering (by myself, thank you) onto the toilet seat, balancing during and after my business, getting back into the wheelchair, and then getting help back into bed. It was exhausting. It was even worse when I was still in Mass General and had staples in my stomach from the exploratory surgery, which I could feel pulling and stretching with every move. There was also the laborious unplugging from tubes and machines. And when you have a small bladder to begin with, it became more trouble than it was worth. Or so I thought. Then my kidneys figured I didn't need them anymore since I wasn't giving them enough fluid to process, and so they shut down entirely.

I had had a room full of visitors who witnessed my hysterics, some of whom had waited several hours for my move to the new Spaulding. Luckily, Jen, the friend whom we had all gathered at Forum to watch finish the Marathon, was there when they told me I had to have the dialysis. She is a nurse at MGH and helped calm me down by offering to go with me to dialysis and then to stay with me for what would be my first night in the new Spaulding.

Thankfully, that one dialysis treatment worked, my kidneys woke back up after their two-week nap, and I became an inveterate water drinker. I settled into my long rehabilitation, physical therapy, and overall adjustment to life on one leg.

Now that I was beginning to feel human again, Mike and a few of my friends took to social media to see if they could find the guy who had held the belt on my leg on Boylston Street. Having established a GoFundMe page to help offset the avalanche of medical bills coming my way, my friends posted on the site that I was looking for my "Guardian Angel." With the miracle that is now our social-media world, within minutes some random stranger posted a picture of Shores holding the tourniquet, and another friend, Carla, then reposted it on Twitter's #Boston.com page with the plea "Please help me locate this Good Samaritan who helped saved my friend Roseann's life." When Kathy Curran, who had interviewed me the week before, saw the post, she reposted it to WCVB's more than one hundred thousand followers on Twitter. The results were nearly instantaneous.

At his parent's house in Reading, Shores's phone buzzed into life with a stream of incoming texts and calls. "Dude! Were you at the marathon? Someone is posting a picture that looks a lot like you. A woman is trying to find her first responder." Soon television camera crews were arriving at his front door, and his name, face, and phone number were flashing on my computer screen.

And with that, I had found him. Later that night, my hands shook as I held the phone, listening to it ring somewhere across town.

"Hello?"

My tears came before my words. Through all of the screams and sirens and panicky voices that I remember that day, his strong, calm voice was unmistakable. I had found the kid who had saved my life.

"Shores? This is Roseann."

••••••

Two days later, my room was unusually crowded. It was Saturday, almost three weeks after the bombing and two days after I had first spoken to Shores on the phone, and my entire world seemed drawn to Room 514. Mom, Dad, Gia, Patrick, my uncle and aunt, Mike, Shana, my girlfriends. They all wanted to meet Shores.

Around 2:00 the room quieted and the crowd parted, and there he was, a shy smile on his face. I reached up as Shores approached the bed, and he leaned in carefully to give me a hug. But the hug lingered, neither of us wanting to let go, and he sat down gently to make it easier for me to hold on. I don't remember ever crying that easily or happily in my life. But that day, that wonderful, wondrous day when Shores reentered my life, I did.

When we finally pulled away, I saw that most eyes in the room were also wet, even stoic Mike's and Shana's, as well as Shores's parents, whom he introduced all around. Bob Salter told me later that it was at that moment that he saw Shores's "funk," as he called it, the two weeks of dark and angry gloom that had settled on his son like a heavy coat, lift. And when it did, a smile returned to Shores's face. Bob reached out and took Lorraine's hand: their son was coming back. He'd be all right.

When all the introductions had been made, Lorraine came over to the side of my bed.

"Thank you for saving my son's life."

I looked up at her in astonishment. "What do you mean? He saved *my* life!"

Lorraine shook her head slowly and smiled. "No, I mean for finding him. He was lost before getting your call, and we

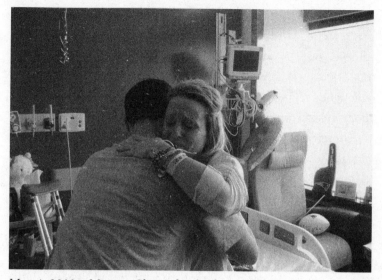

May 4, 2013—Meeting Shores for the first time since the bombing at Spaulding Rehabilitation Hospital.

weren't able to reach him." She looked across the room to where Shores and Gia were talking, my sister wiping tears from her eyes. "Now," Lorraine continued, "it all makes sense. He didn't want to talk about it until he knew if you were okay. Now I think he'll be able to tell us what happened."

Oh, my God, I thought, *he hasn't told them what he did.*

I too looked over at Shores, amazed that the one person who actually had saved my life was the last one to take credit for it.

After he left my room, Shores stopped to properly meet Mike and Shana. Mike clearly remembered the moment on Boylston Street when Shores stepped away from the paddy wagon and the look of pure horror in the young man's eyes. But he also remembered how utterly calm Shores had been. While he was definitely in shock, he was nonetheless unwaveringly in charge of the scene. Mike never questioned for a moment that this kid, whoever he was, knew what he was doing. When he learned that Shores was a twenty-year-old undergrad with absolutely no emergency training, he was floored. He didn't know anything about this kid, but he knew the world needed more just like him.

He put his hand on Shores's shoulder and said, "You did an amazing job holding that tourniquet. Listen, if you need to talk to someone about this, you can call me, okay? Anytime." Shores smiled and nodded but didn't speak. Shana also gave Shores a reassuring embrace.

The story of just what Shores had done in finding me on the street, carrying me to safety, and applying the tourniquet and pressure that saved my life had come out in fits and starts to his family as he struggled through the reality of the situation into which he had been thrust. Bob told me that as a wannabe doctor himself, when he heard that Shores, without any training or experience, had jumped in and done exactly the right thing to save a life, he was stunned. Shores was the hero. Bob had always cherished his son, of course, but after that he saw him with new clarity and new respect.

With Shores finally there, I had looked up at him, Shana, and Mike. It was odd. These three people were really strangers to me; I hadn't known any of them longer than a couple of weeks or spoken more than a few words to them. I barely remembered their names. I had entered Mike into my iPhone contacts as "Matt," even though he had been at the hospital nearly every day. I was still so foggy. And yet, as I lay there, fighting the pain and dull thudding in my head from all the drugs, I felt as comfortable with these three people as with the members of my family who stood nearby. I also realized I felt something else, something that was even better than comfort: safety.

From that moment on, my hospital room felt different, as if we all went from being survivors of a tragedy to comrades after the battle is won. People laughed more freely, and those who had been strangers the day before now hugged and kissed and slapped each other on the back. Even Mom got into it, wrapping them all in her newly instituted bear hugs—Shana, Shores, and Mike—especially Mike.

Shores wasn't the only one for whom a cloud had been lifted. We all felt it, as well as a sense of peace from simply being together.

......

All told, I spent three weeks at the Spaulding Rehabilitation Center in Charlestown, so close to the North End that I could practically see my apartment from my room on the fifth floor. Every day I became more alert and less in pain. And for the most part, I handled the pain well. What I *didn't* handle well was having three different sets of surgery staples taken out in three torturous sessions: from my limb, my left leg's gash wounds, and my stomach, where King had performed a laparoscopy to determine whether I had any shrapnel in my belly. (Fortunately, I didn't—the bruising was probably from the force of the explosion pushing the metal barrier into my abdomen.) Those staple removals hurt as much as anything after the blast had. Because the staples were now intertwined with the nerve endings in my legs and stomach, every one when removed felt like an electric prod into a raw wound. All three times Gia and my friend Nicole had to come with me so I could hold their hands, crushing their fingers to the bone. Even with horse-sized doses of Valium and painkillers, I screamed, I cursed, and I yelled profanities as I never have in my life, before or since. Not my finest hour.

That was my worst actual pain. But when they had to take me off almost all of my medications after the dialysis, the phantom pain in my lost leg became as frustrating as it was unrelenting. Not exactly stinging pain, like the pain of a wound. This pain was more of a hot, tingling feeling where the shin and foot used to be. I've read that your brain remembers the last feeling that the amputated limb had as it was being severed, which explains a lot and makes sense given the lingering pain I felt. I spent many of those days tapping and rubbing my limb, which was supposed to help, but the only thing that did help was the antianxiety, antispasm drug Gabapentin. My anxiety level was pretty good, considering, but the spasms, even though phantom, remained an issue. Once my kidneys were again doing their job and they could tolerate my various medications, the first thing I demanded to have back was my Gabapentin.

My days were a busy blur of appointments, every morning posted on my whiteboard: OT—occupational therapy, PT—physical therapy, and SLP—which I had initially been thrilled to see on the schedule. *Ah!* I thought, *sleep! I love this place. They even schedule naps!* Wrong. What they scheduled was SLP—speech and language pathology. I never asked outright, but I guess they were making sure I didn't have any lingering brain-injury issues around the bomb blast and its potential re-percussive damage to brain tissue. True to form, I was always late for whatever appointment I had. The nurses would arrive with the wheelchair to take me down to therapy, and I'd still be brushing my teeth or trying to get my exercise pants on over my limb without irritating the incision.

"Come on, Roseann, we're gonna be late!" they'd chide.

"Can't you see I only have one leg?" I'd shoot back. That always got a laugh, and I was always forgiven for my tardiness.

During those weeks when I was busy with all the medical, physical, and psychological appointments, I had a welcome stream of visitors. The constant presence of friends and family who had come to Mass General and Spaulding to see me was a source of strength. My "new" room had a million-dollar view of Boston Harbor and the city skyline. Oddly enough, I look back on those weeks now with fondness. I slept better there than I ever have, anywhere, in my entire life. I'd wake up, refreshed, and watch the sun rise over East Boston and the barges and tug-boats making their way in and out of the wharfs that pepper the city's shoreline. Under other circumstances, I could have lived there forever.

That's not to say I didn't have my dark days—I did. I feared I would never again be able to walk on the beach, or swim in the ocean, or bike, or run, or do anything that required two legs. Two real flesh-and-bone legs, not one that weighed ten pounds and was going to require socks and sockets and padding and batteries and computer chips and couldn't be anywhere near the sand or the shore without a lot of mental and physical anguish. I would often get hit by these small but devastating revelations, like I'd probably never be able to wear heels again, something I had *always* worn to add a few inches to my height. And shorts or a bathing suit? Forget it. I couldn't even begin to think about it.

I must have said something to that effect to Mike, or maybe Mom did, because one morning, as I was feeling in a particular funk, the door opened, and there stood Mike, in bathing trunks and a gaudy Hawaiian shirt, an inflatable blue toucan beach floatie around his waist, bright orange water wings on his arms, a *Caddyshack* hat on his head, and a huge beach towel over his shoulder.

"Hey! I hear the pool downstairs is open! Who wants to check it out?"

And here again, in an instant Mike lifted my gloom and replaced it, as he always could, with laughter.

As the days came and went, the conveyer belt of visitors continued, buoying my mood and reminding me how lucky I am to have such wonderful people in my life. Nicole, my friend and coworker, stepped up and became my unofficial lady-in-waiting. Our bosses kindly made sure I had everything I needed, even going so far as to give Nicole time off so that she could be on call to help me out in those early days. She'd do anything, go anywhere, run errands, buy food; you name it, Nicole was on top of it. Our company also gave her enough money to pay for endless pizzas, coffees, and cabs for incoming relatives from the airport. Nicole's staff even contributed money so I could get a badly needed in-room manicure-pedicure (and no, in case you're wondering, I did *not* get a one-foot discount. So unfair!). I was able to get my hairdresser to come and finally rid me of my Don King–esque hair that had been so burned in the blast. Nicole came every day and selflessly gave her time, her energy, and her compassion, easing my anxiety and concern in ways that I can never thank her enough for. And often, at the end of one of these Herculean days, she would go home and bake a batch of not only gluten-free whoopie pies for me but also a regular batch for my visitors, nurses, and doctor.

As I and the other survivors continued to get better and stronger every day, I finally began to grasp the enormity of what had happened, and much of that awareness came from the visitors who came to see us. Our guest list became something of a legend among the Spaulding staff. On any given day you might see star players from the Red Sox, the Bruins, and the Patriots wandering the halls as well as politicians and movie stars sitting on the edge of our beds and posing for selfies. I embarrassed myself at one point by asking to put on Red Sox center fielder Jacoby Ellsbury's World Series ring and not realizing until I had it on my finger that he was looking rather aghast at his prized bling sitting in the crusty soup of my burned hand. Seeing his face, I suggested that maybe I should just keep this one because surely he didn't want it back now, and maybe he could get a replacement? He laughed, and I took it off, gave it a quick little rub on my hospital gown, and handed it back. Kevin Spacey came and gossiped with us about his *House of Cards* shoot, and New England Patriot Rob Gronkowski shyly posed for a picture on the edge of my bed with me and a group of my girlfriends who were hovering and shamelessly flirting with him. And then there was the visit from Teddy Kennedy Jr., son of the late Senator Ted Kennedy.

One gorgeous sunny early-May afternoon, I was sitting outside on the patio overlooking the harbor with a handful of girlfriends when a hospital administrator came out to tell us that Teddy Kennedy was visiting and had asked if he could join us. In all honesty, I didn't know much about him apart from the fact that he had a famous father, but I was always happy to have a visitor. He walked over to us and smiled warmly. We chatted for a few minutes, and when he offered, "You know, we have something in common," I hadn't the faintest clue what he meant. He went on to tell me that he had lost a leg to cancer as a boy. Curious, I asked to see his prosthesis, thinking he would merely roll up his pant leg and give it a tap.

"Sure," he said. He stood up, unbuckled his pants, and, before any of us could speak, dropped them with a resounding clink of his belt buckle on the pavement stones. He stood there in his blue pinstripe boxers.

I was shocked, both by his candor and by the prosthetic leg itself. I had been in Spaulding long enough to have seen scores of prostheses on the other patients and visitors, and this scion of Massachusetts's most illustrious family was standing there on what looked like an antique. It was dented and had repair patches all over it. I couldn't help but ask him why he didn't have the newest and most high-tech prosthetic leg.

He flashed that famous Kennedy smile. "I guess it's like an old pair of broken-in tennis shoes that you really don't want to get rid of because they're so comfortable."

At that precise moment, the president of Spaulding, David Storto, happened by, saw the pants around Kennedy's ankles, and, with his eyebrows raised and his voice full of mischief, said, "Roseann?" As cameras flashed, I could only smile and shrug.

As fun as the celebrity visitors were, I always waited with anticipation for Shores, Shana, and Mike. Mike became such a fixture that I no longer really considered him a visitor. He was just there, quietly guarding me. It struck me how such an imposing man could come and go so quietly. Like a giant shadow. On the days when he didn't visit, I felt his absence and wondered when he was coming back. Shana would come sometimes on her way home from work. She always came into my room with a lot of tough-cop bluster and profanity-laced stories of her latest busts and kept me and whoever else was in the room howling with laughter. She and Mike would fist-bump and grumble about work, and then she would sit on the edge of the bed and ask me how my day was going. She got to know some of the other survivors as well. Sometimes during an evening shift she'd run out for a bite to eat at the Shaw's Supermarket on Border

Street right across the harbor from Spaulding and flash her police lights back at the building as a hello. While she definitely plays the tough cop, she has an incredibly kind heart. On one of her rare days off, she planted a rosebush in her yard in my honor, giving it a silent blessing as she patted the dirt around its base.

Shores wasn't able to visit as often, but of course I didn't blame him. He lived pretty far from Spaulding and was dealing with final exams and the end of the school year. But he made a point of texting me frequently, sending his regards and asking about my progress. Whenever his texts would buzz in on my phone, I couldn't help but feel like a protective older sister or aunt, thinking, *I should be the one checking on him!* When he did visit, we talked easily and laughed a lot.

I'd been at the new Spaulding about a week when we were all offered passes to an upcoming Bruins game by some of the players' wives who lived in the North End. It was a few days away, and I was nervous about venturing out of Spaulding's safety zone, joking that I would go only if they let me ride the Zamboni. Little did I know that we survivors had become minicelebrities, and the following week, my occupational therapist triumphantly announced, "Guess what? I got you on the Zamboni Friday night!"

Damn, I thought, *now I have to go.* But at least I would have Gia and Patrick at my side for the ride to Boston's TD Garden, and Mike, Shores, and Shana would join us there. I'd have all the support I needed. And I did, but even so, I ended up suffering my first real panic attack in the process.

As we got out of the van at the TD Garden, I realized I had no idea how to proceed. I just started hobbling forward on my crutches. Immediately, I was jostled in the rush-hour crowds, my crutches snagged by random bumps and shoulder bags. As we got deeper into the arena, I struggled with every step, and my eyes kept going involuntarily from backpack to backpack, knowing all too well the horror they could contain. I began to feel my heart race and a cold sweat break out under my arms. *If something happens*, I thought, *I will never make it out alive*. I maneuvered myself over to a huge pillar and stood up against it, trying to catch my breath. But as I looked around me, all I could see was a sea of bodies moving in every direction. *Get me out of here!* I wanted to scream, but I managed to keep it together and instead concentrated on breathing and keeping my crutches firmly underneath me until the crowds thinned and I was able to keep moving forward. Thankfully, we had been given access to the Boston Globe's executive suite, and once safely behind that door with the people I knew, I began to breathe easier. Soon Mike and Shana showed up, and just as I settled into my seat overlooking the ice, the door opened, and there stood Shores, beaming. Immediately, I felt not only better but fully relaxed, and for the first time in a long time, life felt normal. This was the first time we four had all met since Shores and I had reconnected, and it just felt right. We were together, drinking beer and watching a game.

I noticed that Shores was a little apprehensive and quiet as he entered the room, not sure how he would fit into this odd little group who had shared so much. But almost as soon as he sat down, he too relaxed, realizing that although there were significant age differences and vastly different life experience among the four of us, we instantly connected.

Everything about the evening was great—until I had to ride the damn Zamboni. They came to get me before the last period, and immediately, I went back into panic mode. Thankfully, my occupational therapist was there, and she helped me get up and on the thing, and when the announcer told the crowd who I was, they went wild. The power of their roar brought tears to my eyes. Feeling their support, their solidarity with me, and with all of us, was overwhelming. This bombing didn't happen just to me; it happened to an entire city, but we weren't going to let it define us. No damn way. As the Zamboni went around and around the rink, I looked up and saw Shores, Shana, and Mike waving madly from the Globe box, and I waved back, my tears blurring their faces.

••••••

My days at Spaulding went by quickly. When I wasn't entertaining my visitors, I was consulting with doctors or struggling through physical therapy. My goal was to get back to normal. I had always loved being outdoors, having the sun on my face and breathing the fresh air. But it was different now. Nothing felt safe. I felt shaky on my crutches on the uneven pavement, unsure navigating curbs, and unsteady getting in and out of cars or up and down off flimsy patio chairs. But my biggest issue was just being outside in the open, vulnerable and visible. I don't think I consciously feared being bombed again, but something about the open air, the endless rooftops around me, the passing boats, even the occasional helicopters and planes in and out of Logan Airport—all suggested possible sniper vantage points to where I sat so exposed, and I didn't like it. But, as with everything else that was awful and uncomfortable and embarrassing about my new life, I set my jaw and told myself, *Just get over it. There's no other way.* When my friends would suggest that we eat lunch outside to enjoy the day, even though my stomach immediately recoiled in dread, I would nod and start gathering myself to follow them out the door. Eventually it got easier, and then, suddenly, one day I forgot to be afraid of going outside. That was the first step in a long recovery. But as my discharge date neared, a whole new fear began to creep in: being on my own.

A month after the bombing, and after three weeks of rehab, my incredible team at Spaulding told me I was ready, physically anyway, to face the world and get back to my life. But I was scared. Just being within Spaulding's walls made me feel safe, knowing that if I needed anything, it was just the click of a buzzer away. How was I possibly going to function on one leg? I live in Boston, a city that has to be one of the least handicapped-friendly cities on earth. The city's subway platforms, walkways, and escalators are hard enough to navigate with two working legs. The elevators and escalators that are in some of the subway stations often break down. Don't even get me started on the uneven brick sidewalks and the parking situation. If you are lucky enough to find a space in a garage without paying a king's ransom, it will probably be a mile away from where you are actually going.

And then there's the weather. Snow and ice in the winter, rain and mud in the spring, and hurricane winds that come in off the Atlantic and barrel between the buildings downtown and the communities where I lived and worked. I was a real estate executive, in and out and up and down stairs and buildings for a living. It all just seemed impossible.

I also wasn't looking forward to being out in the world, where I knew I would be stared at, that my prosthetic leg would be a cause of unwanted attention and pity. The last thing I wanted was *anyone's* pity. No one at Spaulding pitied me. I was just another patient. Out there, it would be "Oh, that *poor girl*." I wasn't sure I could handle it.

Needless to say, there was plenty to make me nervous and frustrated at the thought of resuming my life outside the rehab center. But what really scared me were the fires. I live in the old, cramped North End of Boston. It's not that the neighborhood has more fires than any other, but the ones that we do have are frighteningly close. The North End, while charming and tight-knit and home to some of the best Italian food this side of Rome, is crowded. Most blocks are a long chain of welded-together buildings, and the streets are single-car narrow.

So, when a building goes up in flames, the entire North End can smell the smoke and see the flames lighting up the sky. The thunder of the emergency response is deafening as it echoes through the brick and concrete of the narrow streets and back alleys. Neighbors head out to the streets, praying that the sparks and flames don't spread to their street, and bring water and some-times calzones and espresso to the firefighters. And so someone's personal disaster becomes a sort of strange, sober block party.

One night about six months before the bombing, sirens woke me out of a sound sleep. I smelled smoke, got up, and heard the sirens approaching closer and closer. I saw the fire trucks stop on my street and watched as the building across from mine ex-ploded in flames.

Now, as I contemplated life with one leg, I kept seeing those flames less than a hundred feet away, remembering how fast the building went from having a little smoke trickle out of a first-floor window to all three stories being engulfed in flames, cinders falling against my bedroom window. Minutes. A lot less time than it would take me to wake up, turn on the light, find my prosthesis, put it on, get dressed, climb down my steep stairs, and get out of the building. And if I thought I had it bad, what about Jeff Bauman and Celeste Corcoran and Jessica Kensky, who had all lost *both* of their legs in the bombing? How the hell were they dealing with this new terror of immobility?

I knew I had to face going home, but still, every time I thought about it, a cold feeling sank to the bottom of my stomach. Don't get me wrong—I wanted to go home and get my life back, but this would be my greatest challenge yet.

Mike, having seen fellow soldiers return from deployment in a war zone, knew I was feeling vulnerable. Like many returning soldiers, I had to face life without the usual stuff that you need to feel safe—two working legs, for instance. A day or two before my scheduled discharge, he came into the room with a huge smile on his face and his army helmet on his head. He'd covered it edge to edge with paper flowers and plastic jewels, tiny flip-flops and sunglasses, inflatable floaties like the ones he'd worn to my room a few weeks before, and even tiny bottles of suntan lotion and seashells. This incredible man had gone to the craft store, bought a bag load of these toys, and then spent hours gluing them onto his helmet. For me. Just the thought of him bent over his task, glue gun and plastic jewels in hand, made me smile.

"Anytime you feel scared," he said, a sunflower suddenly dropping from the helmet and falling past his nose and onto his chest, "this helmet will protect you."

The sweetness of his gesture, the sheer silliness of the helmet, and his total ease while looking utterly ridiculous made my heart hiccup in my chest. Who *was* this guy?

The next day, he was rewarded for his kindness: Mom brought a full Italian spread to my room—antipasti, garlic bread, and, for Mike, an entire *pan* of chicken cacciatore, and handed it to him with a smile of such love and thanks that it took my breath away. I didn't know how I felt about this guy yet, but my mother was definitely smitten.

Feeling safe and secure in Mike's Army helmet he decorated for me.

As I had promised myself, I resisted getting into a wheelchair at every opportunity. I knew I had to focus on getting mobile as soon as possible. I was the woman who walked to meet friends for drinks in the neighborhood. I ran along the Charles River. I skied in Maine. I swam on Cape Cod. I toured the Coliseum. I was *that* woman. And I would be again. When I was ready to go home, I was going to walk out the front door on crutches, and once fitted with a prosthesis would ditch the crutches. This was my plan. In some ways, I was still in denial. I still thought of my situation as temporary. Not that my leg would grow back, of course, but that I would continue to recover, get better, and, in the recesses of my mind, somehow get "whole" again. It wouldn't be that easy.

First I had to get out of Spaulding. I had always envisioned that at least Shana and Mike would be there to celebrate the moment. But they were heading out to western Massachusetts where the nonprofit On-Site Academy serves emergency service workers in distress, helping them to regroup, and in some cases rehab, their lives. Even before the bombing, it had been a safe haven for police officers, firefighters, EMTs, and other human service workers who are overwhelmed by the grittier aspects of their jobs. Shana had gone there when she needed to take a break from work, her coworkers, and what had become a nightly routine of going out for a couple of beers with the guys. Those couple of beers had become a six-pack or more, so she had gone to the retreat and gotten herself back on the right path. Now Mike needed to clear his decks and talk in a safe place about what had happened, not only on Boylston Street but on the front lines in Iraq, a subject about which he had never really talked and certainly hadn't yet processed. Mike had come from a long line of firefighters, police, and soldiers, but the bombing had been different for him because it wasn't an accident. It wasn't Iraq and Afghanistan, where risk was assumed every day. And because it was Boston. Along with lives and limbs that were shattered that day was a sense of safety that had been assumed by all Bostonians. We were no longer naive about the brutal dangers of the world, and that reality fell particularly hard on Mike and Shana, both first responders to whatever mayhem befalls their city. Mike in particular couldn't shake his feeling of sadness. He could deal with the dangers he had volunteered for in the army and the fire department. But he had never counted on a war zone coming to his place of work, his home, and affecting average American citizens and children, not soldiers. The bombing had shaken his very foundation and felt like a violation. Unlike his service in Iraq, here he was powerless to strike back, so much so that he even flirted with going back into the military in order to feel that he was *doing* something. Thankfully for me, calmer, saner voices prevailed, and he stayed where he was also needed, helping a one-legged survivor and her family to smile and laugh again.

••••••

I understood all that and was proud of them both for going to the On-Site Academy to take care of themselves, but as I packed my bag and crutched around my room, gathering up the cards and posters and flowers from well-wishers that had collected for weeks, I couldn't help but wish they were there with me. It was a big moment. I was nervous and afraid of what came next, and I didn't have my support system.

Finally, it was time to leave. I slowly crutched my way out of my room, down the elevator to the lobby, and toward the front door. When I turned the corner, I stopped, amazed. There they all were: Shores, Shana, and Mike, beaming and surrounded by my family and friends, reporters, nurses, doctors, and physical therapists, all of whom had helped me to get where I was—standing on my left foot and crutches, not in a wheelchair, *walking* out of there.

As I neared Mike, his face broke into the widest smile I had seen on it since I'd met him. I didn't know he was even capable of a smile that wide and unguarded. His shyness and reserve had always hidden his emotions. With a nervous tickle in my stomach, I smiled back, feeling something I hadn't felt with him before but recognized instantly: true affection. A spark.

On the day of my discharge from Spaulding Rehabilitation Hospital, Mike surprised me. As I went to give him a hug he swept me up off my feet and gave me the biggest bear hug. This is my second favorite photo of the two of us.

The Boston Globe Newspaper, Getty Images

Suddenly, I saw him take a step toward me, sensed what he was planning, and murmured between my teeth, "Don't you dare pick me up." I too, it seemed, had a bit of Mom's disdain for public shows of affection. But Mike didn't seem to care. His smile just got wider, and he swooped me up in his arms and held me in a bear hug as my left foot dangled a good eighteen inches off the floor.

I was as shocked by his exuberant embrace as I was by my own reaction to it: it felt like home.

After saying a few words of thanks at a waiting microphone, I left the building, and another round of congratulatory and teary hugs enveloped me. When I finally extricated myself from the tangle of arms and turned to the curb, what I saw stopped me in my tracks. Two fire engines and a ladder truck, flags flying and lights flashing, were waiting. I looked over at my firefighter. A sly smile pulled at the corners of his mouth.

Mike knew he and Shana had to leave for the retreat, so he had gotten his buddy in the fire department, Lieutenant Glen Martin, to arrange an escort. Fire companies in both Charlestown and the North End wanted to be part of my entourage home.

"The Boston Fire Department brought you to the hospital," Mike said, "and we're going to bring you home." He hugged me again, and with that, he and Shana were off to their retreat in western Massachusetts.

Nearby, Mom got into her car and leaned across the front seat, talking to me through the open passenger window.

"Okay, Roseann, I'll see you soon."

What? I thought. *You're not coming with me, either? You're not going to make sure your daughter who has only one leg and eighteen steep stairs to climb gets settled safely in her apartment?* But I didn't say anything. I knew her limits. This was typical Mom, wanting to avoid a scene, and God forbid a tearful one, at all costs. "Hey," she'd always say in some sort of weird self-defense, "I'm not a caregiver!" So I nodded, afraid I would cry if I spoke, and off she drove, her hand already reaching down to push in the cigarette lighter.

Thankfully, Saint Nicole was there to get me the rest of the way. I maneuvered myself and my crutches into her car, and she started the engine and led the flotilla of trucks away from the curb and away from Spaulding. Tears came to my eyes. I was leaving Spaulding after so much had happened during the three weeks of care—comfort I had felt, and had gotten used to.

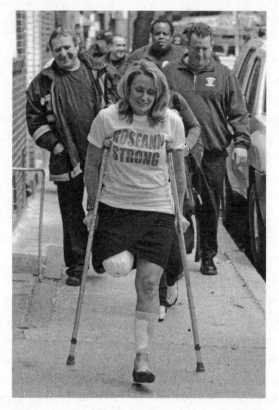

Here I am, for the first time since the bombing, being escorted and assisted to my apartment by the North End's Engine 8 / Ladder 1 Company.

Courtesy of the Boston Herald Newspaper

I had been safe and protected, cared for and supported, even pampered and doted on. As we drove through the Navy Yard, then over the Charlestown Bridge into Boston, I watched the buildings of the North End come into view and the fire trucks inch into the narrow streets of home, and I felt a stirring in my stomach. Fear.

The drive from Spaulding was all too quick. It took only minutes, and before I could get my head around actually going home, Nicole pulled up in front of my apartment. She immediately started unloading my stuff onto the curb while Lieutenant Martin and the other firefighters started taking loads upstairs.

Dear God, my stairs. I live on the second floor with stairs, eighteen of them, so steep and narrow that an elevator couldn't even be installed. Even the able-bodied people in my life comment on how scary they are. It's the kind of staircase that makes it impossible to own a large couch or a side-by-side refrigerator or even a tall bookcase. The stairs themselves are metal with a rubber runner, which should, you'd think, be a good thing for traction. It isn't. Have you ever tried to walk on steep, wet rubber? It's also grooved, and I soon realized that my crutches had a terrifying tendency to catch in the grooves and send me teetering. As a result, in the early days of being home, I resisted coming or going whenever possible. It was just easier to hunker down in my apartment.

Have I mentioned that I have amazing friends? One of them started a page on the "Helping Hands" website so that friends and family could sign up to stay with me at night for my first month home. It was a godsend. But after a month of overnight guests and practically 24-7 help, I knew it was time to at least loosen, if not yet cut, the apron strings and get back to my life.

The day came. It was mid-June, and my last visitor left. I was finally on my own.

chapter nine

ONE STEP AT A TIME

AFTER HAVING ORGANIZED my fire escort from Spaulding, Mike and Shana had climbed into his car for the two-hour drive to western Massachusetts. As Mike started the car, Stevie Wonder's "For Once in My Life" came through the speakers.

Shana rolled her eyes and was about to switch the station when she looked over at Mike. She quickly withdrew her hand. It wasn't the radio; it was coming through the speakers from his iPhone. This was *his* music.

While they had had a handful of conversations in the hallways at Mass General and then Spaulding, she and Mike hadn't really spent much time together, and certainly not enough time for Shana to say what she wanted to say: *Dude! What is this crap? You mean I got two hours of this shit coming my way?*

Usually, Shana drove wherever she was going. Not only did it ease her carsickness but she also didn't trust anyone else behind the wheel. But it was his car, so she had no choice but to sit back and concentrate on not barfing all over it while Stevie, then

Billy Joel, then Bob Seger, then Lionel Richie, and then (*Oh, my God, make it stop!*) Looking Glass's "Brandy" filled the car.

"Not a country fan, huh?" Shana finally asked.

"Nope. Sorry," Mike said, eyes on the road.

"No Tim McGraw, Brad Paisley?" she tried. "Not even Jo Dee Messina?"

"Nope."

Mike drove steadily and smoothly, gently tapping his fingers on the steering wheel and occasionally reaching over to turn the volume up or down. Slowly, ever so slowly, Shana relaxed and, like me, began to feel safe with Mike in charge, even if she was a little nauseated by the drive as much as his choice of music.

As they headed out of Boston and west on the Mass Turnpike, the city faded into the suburbs and then disappeared altogether, replaced by the soft hills and lush forests of western Massachusetts. They talked casually and easily. Mike was relieved to be able to talk to someone outside the fire department about what had happened. While he and his fellow firefighters were a close-knit team, often it was too close, and instead of sharing their feelings of helpless frustration and their sleepless nights after having witnessed Ground Zero of the bombings, most retreated behind the protective masculine walls of "I'm fine; no problem." Mike felt the heavy burden of not having been able to do more for those who had died, and while he suspected his fellow firefighters felt that same weight, they didn't talk about it. There seems to be an unspoken aversion in the fire department to appearing weak. But with Shana, he could share more of what he was going through. They were both civil servants dedicated to protecting the public, and they had similar reactions to the events of the day. As they drove, they talked about the differences and similarities in their jobs, comparing notes and stories and headaches between her life in a blue uniform and his in a red one.

Things were going well until Mike threw his apple core out the window.

"Dude! You did *not* just do that!" Boston police officer Shana Cottone exploded, her head jerking around to watch the core bounce down the road behind them.

Mike looked over at her. "Are you just busting my chops?" he asked, unsure whether to take her seriously.

"If I see that when I'm in my cruiser, I pull the asshole over and make them pick it up!" Even though the apple core was totally biodegradable, Shana says if everybody did it, we'd be driving through a garbage dump of apple cores and banana peels.

Mike chuckled. He could just see her reading the riot act to some poor guy who thought he was basically just feeding the birds or planting an apple tree. "Shana, I just created life; I grew a tree. Circle of life and all that."

Shana folded her arms across her chest, unamused.

"Hey! Look at it this way: we're on our way out to western Mass, home of Johnny Appleseed!"

Nothing.

"Well, you're not in your cruiser, so relax," Mike said, giving up on humor and focusing on the road.

Shana settled back into her seat with a slight grumble and rolled her eyes as she recognized the next song: Whitney Houston's "I Wanna Dance with Somebody." But she felt a soft spot for this guy begin to grow, apple-core-littering scofflaw though he was.

••••••

175

I had only been home a few days when my neighbors in the North End held a benefit Bingo game for me in the Nazarro Center. It was your typical North End afternoon—lots of famous Pizzeria Regina pizza and soda. Mike, who had now returned from his retreat, and Shores, who was making the schlep on the subway, would be there, and I couldn't wait to see them.

Things at the Nazarro Center fund-raiser were going great until I stood to go to the bathroom and got tripped up navigating my crutches through the folding chairs. Next thing I knew, I went down hard, my limb crashing onto the building's cement floor.

Mike and Shores reflexively jumped up and rushed toward me. Before I could wave them off, Gia's husband, Patrick (who hadn't budged an inch off *his* chair, mind you), asked me if I was okay. Catching my breath and rubbing my bruised limb, I nodded yes. He turned back to his pizza and told Mike and Shores over his shoulder, "Don't pick her up. She can get up on her own."

My family *gets* me.

Even though he was forbidden to help me up after watching me crash to the floor in an inglorious heap, Mike was even more watchful for what I might need as I learned to navigate my new world. As it turned out, I needed a hell of a lot, beginning with my fire escape.

"Mike," I said, leaning across the Bingo table after I returned from the bathroom, "would you possibly be able to give me a few instructions on how to get down a fire escape?"

"Absolutely. When do we start?"

And so it began.

We arranged that he would come over the next day, but the fire-escape lesson didn't go as planned, mostly because I was so sore and swollen from my fall at the Nazarro Center. So we ended up sitting around my apartment, ordering lunch, watching television, and talking about whatever came to our minds. We had never had the time or privacy to just sit and talk, and it felt great. I didn't know about him, but I could feel the past two months of stress and anxiety begin to melt off me, and all I wanted to do was curl up and take a nap. It was wonderful to feel normal again, sitting on my couch, surrounded by my things, chatting the afternoon away with Mike.

But a few nights later, I found myself regretting not having spent my time with a Boston fireman more wisely. At 2:00 a.m. I was awakened by my worst nightmare: the smell of smoke. I got up as quickly as I could and crutched from room to room, looking out the windows, sniffing at the door, feeling the walls for heat, trying to determine whether there was a fire and if so, how close it was. Because Mike had urged me to call 911 if I had the slightest doubt about my safety, I did. The firemen, including Mike's buddy Glen Martin, who had escorted me home from Spaulding the week before, came quickly, checked my building and those near me, found nothing, and left. But I wasn't satisfied. Finally, the anxiety growing like a tsunami in my gut, I texted Mike. Given that he was being disturbed in the middle of the night on his day off, he was incredibly sweet.

"You checked the hallway, right?" he texted back. "And there aren't any sirens, right? I'm sure it's just some bozo using a barbeque somewhere he shouldn't."

I told him I couldn't see or hear anything, but still . . .

"Well, do you want me to come over and take a look?"

I knew he was just being nice, and while I didn't want him to feel obligated, the thought of him actually coming over to make sure I was safe, and felt safe, was more than I could resist.

"Would you mind?"

"I'll be there in twenty minutes."

And he was.

Sure enough, by the time he arrived, what was most likely some "bozo's" illegal barbeque or fire pit had died down, and the smell of smoke, while still somewhat evident, was more faint with every passing minute. It made me feel marginally better that it wasn't just my paranoia at work: several of my North End neighbors had also called to report smelling smoke. Lieutenant Martin had a long night responding to our nervous calls.

You'd think I would have been more embarrassed, getting a firefighter out of his bed and across town to check on a nonexistent fire. But all I felt was relief, and safety. Sensing that I wouldn't feel totally at ease for a while, Mike offered to spend the night. I got him sheets and a pillow for the couch, thanked him, and finally got back to bed.

I had my first good night's sleep since returning home.

Mike and I didn't really talk about it, but after that, I think we both realized I needed more time before I would be comfortable on my own. And once again and without being asked, Mike stepped up.

High on my list for getting my life back to normal was finding a prosthetist who would measure, mold, fit, and repeatedly adjust my new prosthetic leg, tailoring it to my body and life. And, as I would soon find out, finding one is not as easy as Googling one.

There are two people who know a female amputee more intimately than any others—her gynecologist and her prosthetist —so choosing this person involved extensive research and interviewing. I had a checklist of thirty questions designed to reveal the candidates' experience, attitude, and approach, everything from their credentials and references to how long and how expensive the visits would be during the protracted fitting process. I was ready.

Mike and I made dates of the appointments—driving around the Boston area to the various prosthetic outfitters, spending upward of two hours with my clipboard of questions, and then stopping for lunch to give us a chance to praise or pulverize the prosthetist. In almost every case, we agreed on whether to thumbs-up or thumbs-down the person. When I finally chose Next Step Bionics and Prosthetics in Newton, Massachusetts, Mike and I soon learned that the appointments had only just begun—the interviewing had been the easy part. Now the seemingly endless fittings began. Even so, I started to look forward to the appointments, not because of the fittings but because I would get to spend almost an entire day with Mike.

On Memorial Day weekend, we decided to drive up to Salem, Massachusetts, for lunch in one of the city's waterfront restaurants. The day was perfect for a drive up the coast, and conversation was light and easy. We talked about our families and friends and the irony of a Yankees and Giants fan finding himself in the heart of Red Sox and Patriots country. We gossiped about what a spectacle the aftermath of the bombing had become. Everyone and their uncle seemed to be taking credit for helping to save survivors, even though many of them had been nowhere near Boston on Marathon Monday.

As we drove back to the city, Mike turned from the wheel and smiled at me. "This has been the most enjoyable Memorial Day I've had in a long time. Thanks."

Mike told me he had lost friends in Iraq and that every year he makes sure to memorialize them. With a shock, I realized that for Mike, Memorial Day wasn't just barbeques and beer and a long weekend near the beach. For him, it was a real *memorial* day, a day about remembering, honoring, and grieving for friends and loved ones. It was about sadness and irretrievable loss. It was about the dignity of service and the grief of death. And it was very, very personal.

And as it had when he had picked me up and given me that bear hug the day I left Spaulding, I felt my heart give a little hitch in my chest. *He's too young*, I told myself, but his attention and concern for every aspect of my safety, the easy conversation, and his killer smile were slowly chipping away at my reserve. While he remained stoically a friend and helpmate, I found myself curious as to whether he was interested in being more. It took a few weeks, but I finally got my chance to ask.

In late June, *People* magazine gathered a handful of the bombing survivors for a photo shoot. Of course, I asked Mike if he would help me get organized and help carry all the bags and accessories that had become part of my routine anytime I had to leave the apartment. Ever since I had left Spaulding, Mike had begun carrying my purse for me, making sure I always had my hands free in order to navigate with my crutches. He did it without a word of complaint or even notice. He just did it, as if it was the most natural thing in the world for a six-foot-one firefighter to carry a woman's purse. Some of his firefighter buddies had seen us at various gatherings, and when they saw him at work, they asked, "Hey, Mike, where's your purse?" True to his nature, Mike dismissed it with a smile and a shrug.

When we got to the photo shoot and I went off to join the other survivors to get ready, the *People* reporter saw him standing there with my purse in one hand and my clothes bag over his shoulder and asked him the nature of our relationship. From where I sat in the photo shoot, I saw them talking, her pen in hand, and as soon as the reporter and I were one on one, I asked

This is one of my favorite photos of us. Mike and I attending a wedding in Vermont over Labor Day Weekend, 2013.

Courtesy of Curran Photography, Burlington, VT

her what she and Mike had talked about. With a sly smile, she suggested I ask him myself.

After our next prosthetic appointment, I decided it was time to find out where I stood with this enigma of a man. Over a lunch of lobsters and clams at Markey's Lobster Pool in Seabrook, New Hampshire, I started in.

"So, I saw that *People* reporter and you talking at the shoot. What did she ask you?"

He hesitated, his fork pausing over his plate, before answering with his typical *no big deal* shrug.

"She wanted to know about us, if we were together, I guess."

"And what did you tell her?" I asked, trying to keep my voice even. I was so nervous that the clam I was shucking nearly got shucked onto the floor.

After one of his long silences, he said with another shrug, "I told her I was your fireman."

Something fluttered through my stomach. After allowing the words to linger in the silence, I asked, "And are you?"

For the first time since our ride in the paddy wagon, he reached over and took my hand. But this time, I didn't have to beg him not to let go.

······

Apart from my medical, physical therapy, media, prosthetic, and business appointments, I began to get back into the world. As I did, I finally began to realize the extent of what had happened. I had been cocooned in Mass General and then Spaulding, really not paying any attention to the international outrage over Boston having been bombed. But once I was back in the world, the magnitude of the attack finally came into focus. T-shirts appeared around the city:

3,520 days to get Osama bin Laden

4 days to get the Tsarnaev brothers

Welcome to Boston!

Another had a picture of a SWAT team hanging off an armored vehicle and bore the words:

National Hide-and-Seek Champions

Boston was very proud that within days it had identified and captured those responsible. Yes, the bastard brothers had succeeded in raining terror down upon an entire city, but they probably hadn't expected what came next: that same city turning to steel in its resolve to bring them to justice for what they had done in and to the heart of Boston.

It was all strange to me, to be part of an international catastrophe, a global conversation. The bombing still felt very personal, and it was. But, like 9/11 and Sandy Hook and Orlando, it was also irrevocably part of a larger history and always would be. I always would be, but I didn't think I would ever get used to it.

Still, I went about normalizing my life and getting back into my social swing, meeting girlfriends for drinks or dinner, taking my nieces to lunch, and getting ready to go back to work. One night, many of us who had been part of my experience that day on Boylston Street gathered at a local restaurant, Antico Forno in the North End: Sabrina, Jenna, Megan, Alissa, Jen, Johnny Abbott and his wife, Shores, Shana, Mike, and me. Having those core people together, those closest to what had happened, allowed us all to celebrate moving forward and not have to explain, to simply share an evening without talking about where we were in the tragedy. We all already knew.

As we were getting situated and the waiter was handing out menus, someone, Jenna, I think, jumped in and asked if they had a gluten-free menu for me.

"She's gluten-intolerant," Jenna added, just in case the man didn't get it.

"Excuse me," I said, hoping my voice was more sarcastic than angry, "I lost my leg, not my voice."

Jenna meant well, but the kid gloves everybody was using around me were beginning to chafe. I know everybody was just trying to be there if and when I needed help, but their concern often made me feel constrained, even claustrophobic. Most days I responded to their helicopter hovering with humor.

A few days after our big dinner in the North End, Jen and I went to replace my sunglasses, which had been blown off my face by the bomb. The chirpy salesgirl at the Sunglass Hut on Newbury Street was visibly nervous when she watched me crutch into the store on only one leg. I explained that I was there to replace my Ray-Bans.

"Bummer!" she said, oozing with over-the-top empathy. "Like, when did you lose your sunglasses?"

"The same day I lost my leg."

"You did *not* just say that!" Jen said, mortified for the poor girl. I laughed, hoping to show that I meant it as a joke, but it was too late. I probably should have stopped myself because the salesgirl was clearly out of her element in how to deal with me and quickly fluttered off to help another customer in the store.

At one point, a know-it-all reporter commented on my drinking a Diet Coke during an interview.

"That stuff is poison," she said. "It could literally kill you."

I looked at her hard, taking a breath before answering. "You know, I gave up diet soda for a year. And then I got blown up, so I said, 'Fuck it. I'm drinking the Diet Coke.'"

That shut her up.

But sometimes humor didn't work and everybody's "helpful" suggestions just felt patronizing. One particularly tough afternoon, I sat down and started writing a list of "Things I Hate," hoping that getting them out on paper would be cathartic. I hate when people call me a hero or tell me they're proud of me—for what? Losing a leg? Then there are the people with two functioning legs trying to give me advice about my one-legged experience, and others who see my prosthesis and tell me how they *too* once had knee surgery or their leg in a brace, to which I answer, "Lucky you." And while I do know they're only trying to be nice, when people look down at my real and prosthetic legs, they feel compelled to say something and end up complimenting my shoes or toenail polish. *Really?* I also hate how clumsy I feel with the ten-pound weight attached to my body. And the fact that I can't just "throw on" a pair of flip-flops and run out the door. I have to sit down to put on a pair of sensible shoes that I will be sure won't slide off without my even knowing it.

••••••

I was the same person I had been before I lost a leg. I struggled every day to get on with my life, as normal a life as I could make it. But every time someone fussed or fretted over me in a way they never had before April 15, it just served to remind me that I wasn't normal in their eyes and might never be again.

The three people from whom I never had to worry about getting special treatment were Mike, Shana, and Shores. After leaving Spaulding, and with Mike more and more a fixture in my life, we found every excuse to call Shana and Shores to see if they could join us at various events or for drinks or dinner. Soon we didn't need an excuse and would get together whenever our schedules allowed. While we all enjoyed just hanging out, I also found a rare comfort in being able to be myself, without explanation or excuse for the catastrophic changes that had occurred a couple of months before. Mike in particular always found ways to remind me that shit happens, but you have to keep moving and try to laugh along the way. Mike and Shana called me "the one-legger" and would tease me about the e-mails I'd get from anonymous "stump devotees," people with a sexual fetish involving amputees (who the hell ever *heard* of such a thing?). Whenever we gathered, usually over a dinner of beer and pizza, the conversation never focused on me and my leg, or Shores and his heroism, or the bombers and their trial. While we acknowledged the catastrophe that had brought us together, our friendship was really based on easy conversation, shared senses of humor, and true affection for each other. In my case, it was also about being around the few people who made me feel safe. Also, we all shared a similar perspective on the tragedy—we would not make it the focal point of our lives. We would look forward to the future and not dwell in the past. In the wake of the bombing, we had all become unintentional celebrities, hounded by media and compelled to tell and retell the story of the worst day of our lives in excruciating detail. We were all exhausted by it—the attention, the notoriety, and the sheer sadness of what had happened to us. While we knew we couldn't escape it entirely, we did find solace whenever we were together in being able to be who we had been *before* the bombing.

We often joke about the fact that if not for the bombing, we four would never have become friends. We're only human, and we all tend to make snap judgments of others. Shores might have seemed like just a trust-fund millennial, Shana a stereotypical gruff cop, Mike an unemotional man's man, and I some sort of party girl. We laugh now about how we would have seen each other from a dispassionate distance, but it's absolutely true. Boston can be a very self-segregating town.

I thanked the powers that be every day that we did meet each other, and when we got together for drinks or dinner, instead of dwelling on the elephant in the room, we talked about Shores's final exams and the cases Shana was working and Mike being called to an elderly woman's house because she couldn't get her prescription bottle open. I loved those evenings because no one felt self-conscious around me or apologized for bumping my chair. I watched Mike gently scold Shores for goofing off before an exam and Shana give Mike a not-so-gentle elbow in the ribs for a joke he made about lesbians. They were, in a word, becoming like family.

chapter ten

GENIE—THE NEW NORMAL

THE MOMENT WHEN I was finally able to stand up, without crutches and on two legs, I cried. Looking down and standing on two feet was completely overwhelming—in the best and worst sense of the word.

After what seemed like a million fittings for the socket and the prosthesis, my leg finally arrived. Driving over to get it attached, I was nervous, as if I were on my way to a very bizarre blind date. What if I didn't like it? What if it just didn't fit? What if the design I had picked weeks ago no longer was right?

But once I arrived, there it was, being carried into the room by my prosthetist, Arthur Graham, followed by his team of engineers and designers, who would help with the fitting. After getting my limb properly suited up in its socklike silicone liner and then a thick rubber cup that was placed around the end to anchor it in the socket, I stood on my left leg, balanced over the socket's wide opening at the top of the prosthesis, and slid my limb in. After some light hops to force the suction cup down deep into the bottom of the socket, I found myself standing on my right leg for the first time since April 15, almost exactly two months earlier.

It was an incredible moment for me, but it was also bittersweet. And final. Not that I ever thought, *Hey, maybe the leg will miraculously regenerate!* Or *Maybe this is a nightmare, and I'm going to wake up with two legs.* But standing there looking down at this new, hideously ugly, deadweight imitation of my leg was sobering. And it was forever.

I named her Genie, after her model type—Genium. State-of-the-art robotics, baby. But twenty-first-century robotics or not, the truth is, prostheses suck. Truly suck. On bad days, her name was Fucker, for obvious reasons. But at least it was better than what amputees had had to deal with in previous centuries. As with so much of human history, the advancement of prosthetic arms and legs corresponded to the progression of wars, and with them the huge increases in the number of traumatic amputations. Never has that been more true than in the years during and after World Wars I and II, Vietnam, and more recently Iraq and Afghanistan. Those wars brought with them the widespread use of a previously isolated weapon: the IED. With tens of thousands of veterans from the Iraq and Afghanistan wars suffering wounds, over 1,600 of them traumatic amputations, the sudden need for better and more readily available prosthetic devices was urgent. Soon, with enormous funding coming primarily from the Department of Defense, prostheses went from being merely functional to state-of-the-art. One robotic arm, for instance, is named after Luke Skywalker for its ability to pick up coins and peel a grape. Interestingly, the premier supplier of prosthetic devices is not an American company; it's German, founded in 1919 by a man named Otto Bock to develop products for the soldiers returning from World War I. The two models I have had, the Genium and then the X3, are their top-shelf prostheses. So I guess if I was going to lose a leg, this is the best time to do it. But that still doesn't make it better than my actual leg.

One of the not-so-fun challenges faced by a woman who lives with a prosthetic leg is using the bathroom. The first time I peed *in* my prosthetic leg, I cried. I'm not crystal clear on whether the accident was a matter of bad aim or bad timing, but the few times that I've peed in my leg, it was primarily the fault of a wide and slick plastic toilet seat, which makes it difficult to keep the prosthesis from slipping around. Even in the past, whenever I had been forced to pee in the bushes during a road trip or while hiking or camping, let's just say that more than once I came away with wet socks, so aim is definitely an issue for me. Genie didn't make things better. Something about the seat's width, my crooked stream, and the socket of Genie's upper inside lip being less than an inch from the source occasionally combined for a wet prosthesis and a puddle on the bathroom floor. I've had to pour my own pee out of my prosthetic leg before returning to the party or restaurant table. But I don't blame Genie. Back then, she and I were just getting to know each other.

I am known in this new prosthetic world of mine as an above-the-knee amputee, or AK. We AKs sometimes call those whose legs were amputated below the knee "BKs" or "paper cuts." I know it sounds harsh, but it's only because we have to have a sense of humor about our situation. Otherwise we'd lose our minds. I never thought I would envy any amputee, but I would trade places in a heartbeat with someone who still has their knee. Not only is their recovery months, even years, faster but their mobility and security on their prosthesis are light years better than they are for us AKs. They know where they're putting their foot because it's steered by the knee. Further, they have a solid thigh and knee to support their weight on their prosthetic foot, while we have an atrophied limb suspended in the socket (not touching its base), and the minute you sweat, it's no longer snug and instead slips and slides around inside the socket. And that's when the blisters start.

Here's an exercise for you. Try to imagine putting your leg into a long pipe, wide enough to fit snugly around your upper thigh. The tube has to be long enough that your foot dangles inside it but does not touch the floor. The top end of the tube has a hard, thick plastic lip, the edges of which fit firmly, very firmly, up under your pubic bone and against your butt. Now put all of your weight on that plastic lip digging into your groin and take a step. Now try to imagine walking up a flight of stairs. First, you lift the ten-pound "pipe," not with your foot or your knee (which aren't there anymore) or even your thigh but by thrusting the "pipe" back with a hard snap of your hip flexor, then using that momentum to quickly snap it forward and up onto the stair. Then, praying the robotic knee has in fact locked into place, you put your full weight on it and step up, then step up with the "good" leg. That's one stair. A flight of five or six stairs leaves me sweating and out of breath as if I've run a mile on the beach dragging a tire through the deep sand. "Paper cuts" simply lift their thigh, bend the knee that's still there, place their *four*-pound prosthetic foot on the stair, and step up.

Beyond the exhaustion of learning how to maneuver the deadweight on the end of my body, there is my ever-present terror of smelling smoke, the frustration of snow and ice underfoot, and the simple dread of having to make it to the bathroom fast. There is no such thing as fast in my world anymore. Between me and the toilet in the middle of the night, with my leg off for sleeping, there are the obstacles of crutches and darkness.

Then there are the sheer mechanics of the thing. My prosthesis needs a tune-up at least once a year. The tune-ups take upward of a month, so for that month I am on a loaner leg, praying *it* doesn't break down.

The leg's knee has a microprocessor in it along with a gyroscope, both of which help monitor and mimic what my flesh-and-bone left leg is doing. If it's going up or down an incline, the computer will adjust the right prosthetic knee to simulate what that left knee is doing. The prosthetic knee will tighten and loosen in relation to the left leg so that it does not lock in place or collapse underneath me. It is not fail-proof (or fall-proof), as it has collapsed and I have fallen, but thankfully, it tends to be a slow-motion fall, and I can usually catch myself. (When a regular mechanical knee, which operates more like a basic hinge, collapses, it does so without warning, and I don't know I'm falling until I am lying on my back and looking up at the sky.) That computer runs on a battery, so I have to plug in my leg every night and hope that in the morning, it will function correctly. Sometimes it doesn't. Sometimes it won't stop beeping and vibrating, like a pocket pager gone psycho, or the robotic knee refuses to bend and I have to swing the stiff leg to walk and manually bend it when I sit down.

While today's prostheses look better than they used to, they are still just downright ugly, heavy, and clunky. The entire world stares at it, at me, with unabashed curiosity and sometimes fear, as if losing a limb is contagious. All that gaping sometimes is accompanied by judgment. When I am sitting behind the wheel of my car, there is no way to tell that I have a prosthetic leg. One day, I pulled into a handicapped space on a crowded street in a popular tourist town on Cape Cod. As I did, a man eating an ice-cream cone must have assumed I was some ditzy blonde bogarting the space for a jaunt into the nearby Lilly Pulitzer store. He sat there with his ice-cream cone, slowly shaking his head from side to side as if to say, "Shame on you, young lady." I felt a cold rage bubble up in my chest, and before I knew it, I was out of the car and yelling across the street at him.

"What? Why are you shaking your head at me?" I demanded, hot with anger.

The man, who couldn't have missed my prosthetic leg after I slid out of the car in my summer shorts, was instantly red-faced and quietly said, "No, I wasn't."

"Yeah! You were!" I shouted back.

I'm not proud of the moment. The man was elderly, and I shouldn't have gone off on him. We all judge people—*I* judge people—so calling him out on his judgment of me didn't make me feel any better; I only felt a sad guilt. But sometimes the frustration of having strangers gape, and point, and judge, and *misjudge* gets the better of me.

Right after I got Genie, and for several months while I gained confidence walking on her, my eyes were trained on the ground in front of me, not on the faces around me. I missed, therefore, the stares and pointing that Mike and my friends and family witnessed on a daily basis. My only awareness would be when one of my friends would suddenly blurt, "Yeah! It's a fake leg! Take a good look, buddy!" One night Mike and I were walking through a crowded restaurant, and some drunk jerk yelled, "Make way! We got a handicapped person coming through!" Without missing a beat, Mike retorted, "She's handi-CAPABLE!" smiling at his own joke, even if it was entirely missed by the drunk.

But even in those instances, I remained focused on not tripping on a table leg or a curb. In time, as I got more confident, my eyes finally started focusing on what was in front of me. That was when I started noticing the stares, and I began to feel angry.

Don't get me wrong; I love my prosthesis. Actually, "love" might be a bit much. Let's just say we accept each other. But I do appreciate the fact that I am even able to wear it. Many amputees are so badly injured that they can't tolerate a prosthesis: either they are missing all of their leg, right up to their pelvic bone, or their associated injuries, like burns and skin grafts, would be aggravated by a prosthesis. And then there are those who don't have good, or in some cases any, insurance and are left with practically prehistoric prosthetic limbs.

Not only is my state-of-the-art prosthesis waterproof and computerized, but it's not my only one. I also have a running "blade" leg, a biking leg, and, yes, a "cosmetic," or dress-up, leg, which matches my real leg with somewhat eerie silicone perfection for when I want to wear a skirt or shorts and not be a curiosity for those around me. I appreciate the legs because they keep me out of a wheelchair; they allow me to walk to lunch with my girlfriends on the narrow, crowded North End streets that would be nearly impossible in a wheelchair; and they afford a sense of mobility, and of safety, if I ever need to move away from danger relatively quickly. I used to walk home from my neighborhood bars and restaurants and friends' apartments and think nothing of it. Now my inability to truly run from trouble has hindered that freedom. Perhaps after years of walking and running on my prostheses, I will regain my confidence, but for now, it's gone.

This has all been tough, but it could have been so much worse. I'm alive. I and sixteen other people lost our limbs in an international spectacle that forever became part of our collective history. The response was global, and we all have been recipients of an outpouring of financial and emotional support that few amputees ever receive. In part because of the high-profile nature of the bombing, several insurance companies stepped up and provided us with coverage that the average amputee never sees. While I am grateful for the assistance, I am also keenly aware of the disparity and do my best to assist other amputees in fighting for their proper coverage after the calamitous loss of a limb. I speak to organizations aimed at bettering the lives of those facing similar situations and help to provide resources. But the most important thing I tell other amputees is that they have to learn to be advocates for themselves.

••••••

As the summer of 2013 turned to fall, I slowly felt myself easing back into a routine, into my life. Unfortunately, one thing that stayed frustratingly the same after the bombing was the despair of standing in front of my closet. Trying to find outfits that make me feel pretty and fashionable has never been easy for me. I've always hated shopping. I don't have the kind of body on which clothes fit easily and look great. When I was a girl, I was diagnosed with scoliosis and had a back brace that I was supposed to wear twenty-three hours a day. And not some around-the-lower-back kind of brace; this was a hard plastic suit of armor that went from my hip bone to right under my arms and was tightened with a series of thick nylon straps, the buckles pinching my skin every time I put it on—kind of like a Styrofoam corset. Try looking cute and stylish with a quarter-inch layer of plastic under your tank top and shorts. Although it ended up on the floor more than on my body, I wore that medieval contraption for a while. No sooner was I out of it than puberty hit, and with it came the DD breasts, which were so uncomfortably oversized for my five-foot-one-inch body that, years later, I had them surgically reduced. Every time I went shopping, I would cry in dressing rooms, a pile of size-large blouses at my feet: even they didn't fit. Removing the four pounds of excess flesh and going from a DD to a C cup felt like I was unzipping a bodysuit, like the one Robin Williams wore in *Mrs. Doubtfire*, and stepping out, leaving all that excess baggage on the floor.

But, while I could surgically remove the excess pounds from my chest, it was not so easily done with the rest of the extra pesky pounds on my body. Like many women, I have always had issues with the way my body looks. Even before the bombing, getting dressed had been fraught for me. Now, not only did everything take at least twice as long to do—shower, makeup, hair, breakfast—on top of it all, I'd spend what felt like hours standing in front of my closet, fighting tears and trying to find something to wear. None of my clothes fit like they used to, and some I couldn't wear at all. Not only had I not been to the gym in months, but Genie's socket on the inside comes right up to my groin and on the outside comes right up to my hip, creating a large, hard ridge and making skinny jeans or tight leggings and even most skirts uncomfortable, if not impossible, to wear without constant adjusting and fidgeting. The clothes staring back at me from the closet were a sad reminder of the life I used to have.

But it was the shoes that really broke my heart. Rows of strappy sandals and platform wedges and spiky heels—cruel little size-eight reminders gathering dust. The day before the marathon, I had gone shopping for clothes I was going to wear to Cancún. I bought a pair of platform sandals to wear dancing at the beachfront bars at night. Two years later, the box still sits on the shelf, the sandals unworn.

Most mornings I'd just grab something, anything, to wear and get on with my day. I had to constantly remind myself that at least I was walking, and without a wheelchair or even crutches. My personal trainer, whom I had been working with for years, retrained himself to work with prostheses, and every day my gait became, if not graceful, at least more my own. Genie and I learned to navigate my apartment's hellish stairs, and I once again could spontaneously meet friends around the corner for a drink or a bite to eat without having to preplan it hours or days in advance.

Even though walking on a prosthesis allowed me some freedom, traveling anywhere now demanded a laundry list of infrastructure: extra socks for my limb, maybe another leg—what if I wanted to take a short jog or maybe get on a stationary bike?—crutches for getting up in the middle of the night, suitcase, and a shower chair.

I hate the shower chair. I hate that I need it. I never feel quite so handicapped as when I sit in the shower, like an old lady in a nursing home or, well, a forty-five-year-old woman with one leg. I used to love long, luxurious showers, but now I can't get out of there fast enough.

One morning after Mike spent the night, I couldn't help but notice that his shower was long enough to drain the Quabbin Reservoir. He was taking just as long, if not longer, than I had, and he had two legs and no hair to shampoo! What the hell? When I couldn't stand it any longer, I asked through the door, "What *are* you doing in there?"

The door opened. After the steam cleared, Mike stood there, a towel around his waist, smiling. "Taking a shower," he answered with his usual exactness.

"Yes, I know, but my God! Twenty minutes?"

He reached up to wipe the steam off the mirror.

"I just love that chair. I can relax, shave my head, clip my nails; it's like a steam bath. It's great."

And there you have it. One woman's nemesis is another man's gift from the shower gods. I still didn't love the chair, but I loved that he did and even found myself appreciating it just a little.

••••••

Ever since the bombing thrust me and the other survivors into the public eye, I had to get used to being a recognizable figure. It did not dawn on me until after I'd given a few interviews how much of my personal life would be out there in the media. I had always been able to control my environment and had lived a quiet, private life. But that went out the window. It seemed as if overnight my e-mail and voice mail were full with invitations from organizations and corporate meetings, all wanting to hear about my experience as a survivor of the bombing and several hoping to help me return to a "new normal." Organizations geared toward supporting the disabled reached out to me to join their various gatherings. And even though traveling now would be much more difficult, I tried to say yes to everything. In order to do so, I learned how to schlep my carry-on luggage, including my extra leg in its bag, and get it into the overhead compartment, how to navigate the occasional broken elevator or escalator, and how to anticipate and overcome an endless list of new obstacles. I needed to get back into the world, and this seemed like a perfect way to do it. That is, as long as Mike could go with me. Having him there to help me and keep me safe made it all possible, especially in the first few weeks and months after I left Spaulding.

Through it all, Mike was by my side, making me laugh. When I reached for Genie in the morning, I would often find her full of M&Ms, an orange, a penny candy, or some of his leftover craft-store items—tiny flip-flops and paper flowers and paste-on jewels.

Mike made life better just by being there. From the first day that he told me he was my fireman, we began the delicate work of becoming a couple. Like any relationship, it isn't always easy. He and I are very different people. He enjoys a quiet night at home, watching a game and sharing a pizza (that man can eat pizza three meals a day, seven days a week); I am much more social, always up for a night out with friends. On the rare occasions when we argue, he needs to think and mull over an issue, while I prefer to just address it once, let it go, and move on. But as we've grown together, we've learned how to work with each other, and it just keeps getting better and better.

So, back out into the world I went, with Mike at my side.

chapter eleven

TWO STEPS FORWARD, ONE OR TWO BACK

BY LATE SEPTEMBER, I decided to go back to work. My bosses at National Development had been amazing throughout my recovery, assuring me that I could take as long as I needed. But after nearly six months, it was time to get back in the saddle.

First I practiced for and took a one-legged driving test. After a few test drives around a parking lot, I got into my car and drove to work on October 1, 2013.

My coworkers were wonderful. They did everything they could to ease my transition back to work and bring me fully up to speed with my twenty-five-person team. Unfortunately, they did too much. I literally never had to leave my chair. "Roseann, let me get you some tea." "What can I bring you for lunch?" "Here, I can make those copies." "Let me get this for you . . ." and on and on. I had spent hundreds of painful hours in the gym, trying to regain strength and agility, and as I sat and watched, all that progress from working with both a physical therapist and a personal trainer was practically squandered in a matter of days. At first I tried to resist their offers, but after a while it became easier to just let them do it and not have to do the back-and-forth myself. Soon my already ill-fitting clothes were tight in all the wrong places, and the inactivity began to wear on my psyche. It wasn't good. It still isn't, actually. But I kept at it. I had always worked. Always. I was not going to let that change.

In early November, we were all invited to celebrate Shores's twenty-first birthday with his friends and extended family in Reading. Shana, Mike, and I raised our glasses to the now legal Shores, who was then the center of some drinking game involving a mason jar of alcohol passed among the other twentysomethings around the kitchen island. I can't remember the details of the game, but I *do* remember Lorraine's scrumptious home cooking, including the family favorite, lobster macaroni and cheese, as well as chicken *and* eggplant parmesan and enough salads to satisfy every vegetarian east of Chicago. Shana is still talking about the food from that day.

As Thanksgiving 2013 approached, it didn't feel right to celebrate without all of those for whom I was so grateful. So in addition to Gia and Patrick and their girls, and Mom and Mom's boyfriend, Donald, I reached out to Mike, Shana, and Shores and insisted that they join us at Mom's and bring their families to the feast. While Shores was otherwise spoken for at his family's house in Reading, Shana and her sister came, and of course Mike.

Once we were all seated at an assortment of folding tables, I looked across the room at the wild, wonderful, crazy mixture of faces and voices and stood to say a few words of welcome. I looked at Mike and Shana, Mike of course sitting back and quietly observing the conversation at his table and Shana holding court with one of her loud, hysterical stories about patrolling the streets of Boston, and I gave a quiet prayer of thanks. My God, how my life had changed since my last Thanksgiving—in every possible way. I had been brought back from the dead, was navigating life with a new leg and a new love, and was getting to know an entirely new branch of my already crazy family.

"Thank you all," I began, my voice already cracking and my eyes tearing up. I cleared my throat and began again. "Thank you for being here. And thank you for having been here for me for the past seven months. I can't imagine any of this without each and every one of you. I don't know how the other survivors are feeling today, but I can tell you that I feel like the luckiest woman on Earth to be here, to be alive, and to be with all of you."

Even Mom had a tear in her eye.

Earlier in the year, Mom had spoken at a fund-raiser my Uncle Bill, her brother, and some of his buddies had organized for me in Dracut. More than three hundred people showed up, including Dad and Lennie. Shores and his girlfriend came, as did Shana and hers, and of course Mike. After months of keeping Mom on a "need-to-know" basis about me and Mike, I pulled her aside at the event and finally told her we were dating. She had been so pushy about it, I guess I didn't want to tell her until he and I had figured things out a little more. I also didn't want her to become even more attached to Mike than she already was in case it didn't work out. As I had suspected she would be, she was genuinely thrilled for me.

After a silent auction and cocktail hour, people settled into their seats for dinner. Mom rose from her chair, and someone near her clinked a glass for silence.

"As most of you know, I am Roseann's mother."

Mom spoke as I've never heard her speak before. Although she never shed a tear, her voice cracked with emotion but remained powerful and defiant. She spoke of my experience and my survival and how life is about friendship and love and support. She spoke simply but forcefully, quoting Carole King's "You've Got a Friend," saying she knew that I would always be surrounded by friends and never have to walk alone. And then, turning to Mike, Shana, and Shores, she gave tribute to those who had been there and helped save my life.

If I was astonished at her words, their effect was even more astounding to those around me. Sitting at the head table, I watched Shores bow his head, then wipe a tear or two, and then put his head in his hands and weep. In all of the months since the attack and all of our gatherings, Shores had always put on a brave face, not really exploring his deeper emotions about the bombing and his miraculous actions in saving my life. While I was sure he was struggling, he nevertheless always behaved like our cheerful younger brother. He told me once that emotional displays are not his "thing." But here he was, allowing Mom's words to wash over him. I asked him later why her words hit him so hard, and he said simply, "I realized how close we all came that day, and how if I had been just a few feet from where I was, it could have been my mother giving that speech. And, let's face it," he added with a smile, "your mom isn't one to go soft. And yet there she was speaking so powerfully about how much she loves you and how we all are part of you being here." Even retelling the story, he had to stop to collect himself. "I guess I'm proud of that."

As I watched Shores share his tears with us, I realized that he and I and Shana and Mike and all the people they brought with them were becoming another family, a new fabric that comforts and protects, shapes and defines who we are in the world. In the months after the marathon, I think I worried that Mike, Shana, Shores, and I were all somehow experiencing a shipboard romance and that our love for each other would fade with time. But it did just the opposite. It grew stronger. And I realized that it wasn't the atrocity of the event that had drawn us together; it was the fierce, almost animal instinct to protect each other. Between Shana's expletive-laced language and tender heart and Shores's old-soul dearness and young passion and, of course, Mike's quiet protection and intense love for us all, we were drawn to each other and became a tribe of four unlikely comrades of the same battle.

While that new tribe, as well as my increasing sense of freedom, was redefining my life in wonderful ways every day, one thing wasn't: work. That wasn't getting any better. It was my own fault, but between not leaving my chair because everybody did everything for me and their constantly bringing me food and treats, I felt like the proverbial beached whale. It didn't help that I kept tripping, usually catching myself but once taking a spectacular fall, the stack of papers in my hand fluttering down around me as I lay on the floor. It was as painful as it was embarrassing and depressing. Soon it seemed as if I was taking more days off than going in, and I began to realize that, for the time being at least, it was going to be impossible to do my job, to manage my team, and to fulfill my responsibilities to finish the company's latest huge project.

By Christmas, I had a bigger worry than how to do my job: the weather. The winter of 2013–2014 began with the first snow of the year in mid-November, and by Christmas, we Bostonians were already sick of it. Romantic white Christmas or not, we had had enough. Unlike the picture-postcard New England towns, covered in a cozy layer of pristine white snow, with old pickup trucks parked outside farmhouses and wreaths hanging in the six-pane windows, after the first hours of a snowfall in the city, it becomes a pain in the butt. Not only is there nowhere to put it, but few apartment-building residents bother to take on the onerous task of shoveling the walk, leaving it to some other tenant—a tenant with a shovel, say. It's the landlord's responsibility, but Boston has more absentee landlords than traffic jams. And in the North End, even if someone shoveled, they'd have to shovel it into the street, and then the snowplow would come along and push it all back onto the sidewalks. So as I sat and watched storm after storm descend on Boston, dumping a foot of snow at a time, I became a prisoner in my own apartment. Even if I braved the sidewalk in front of my house, which I could see from the living room more often than not had not been shoveled, I had the crosswalk to contend with. Ask any Bostonian, and they will tell you that during the winter months, everyone becomes a very good hurdle jumper in order to navigate the snowbanks, slushy puddles, and ice. Not me. Weeks went by, and in I stayed. One day my cabin fever got so bad that I opened my bedroom window and stuck my head out just to feel the snow on my face.

It didn't help that the winter of 2013–2014 was one of the snowiest in history, rivaling 1978 and its record-breaking blizzard, so the streets of the North End, of the entire city, really, might just as well have been cliffs in the Grand Canyon. For me, they were equally nonnegotiable.

The new year, 2014, brought with it a bucketload of new challenges, from an operation on one of my blown eardrums, which caused a lot of pain but didn't do much to improve my hearing, to the continued task of desperately trying to get back into the swing of things at work. Thankfully, my friends and Mike kept me from losing my mind. But sometimes they couldn't prevent my simple sadness. In February, *Runners' World* magazine called to say they were doing an article and photo spread featuring some Boston Marathon legends, like Bill Rodgers and Dave McGillivray. They wanted a few of the survivors to tell our inspiring stories on the one-year anniversary.

I had hoped I would be able to run the Boston Athletic Association's 5K, traditionally run the day before the actual marathon. I thought that by April 2014, I would be physically ready and able to do it, but I totally underestimated the logistics of learning how to run on a prosthetic blade. I had had a grandiose idea that when I got the blade, I would be able to just strap it on and go out and run the five kilometers. But instead I learned a sad reality: I needed to learn how to walk before I could run. So instead of training for the race, I was just depressed. Not only was five kilometers beyond my reach, but my friend Sabrina was following through on our marathon-day promise to "run it next year," and I was having to watch from the sidelines. Seeing her train and get more and more excited about running the race filled me with a lonely, even jealous, ache.

So I almost felt like I should tell the *Runners' World* reporter that my progress probably wouldn't do much inspiring. But I agreed to do the article. Later that week, I stood with others who had been at the bombing, some survivors (although I was the only amputee) but mostly those who had suffered some hearing damage or shrapnel wounds or had had shrapnel embedded in their clothing or shoes. Listening to their chatter, my heart sank. Honestly, I'd had no idea how much it would bother me to hear all of these people getting ready to run again while I was barely able to walk. Standing there for the photo shoot, I couldn't escape their running talk, and I felt myself sink deeper and deeper into a sadness that stayed with me for months.

"I'm finally running again in shorts," said one woman whose lower leg had been hit by shrapnel. "I refuse to let my scars keep me back."

Another chimed in, "Me too! It's been tough with the ringing in my ears to regain my balance, but I'm back at it."

Another offered that he'd "never stopped running." I wanted to ask, *Why would you have to with just a blown eardrum?* but kept my sour grapes to myself.

Don't get me wrong. I was happy for those people that they could run. I just wished I was one of them.

In the weeks and months since the bombing, I had felt a growing discomfort with these so-called survivors. In my mind, I thought of them more as *witnesses* than as survivors; I had difficulty lumping everyone together with those who had lost their lives or those of us who had fought to stay alive. It was simply hard to hear. In addition to feeling frustrated, I left the photo shoot feeling fat and discouraged. Not only was I *not* running the marathon in a few months, but I could barely walk a city block without getting winded and my prosthesis chafing my limb. I tried not to resent those with lesser injuries, but it wasn't easy.

And then, in late March, something happened that jolted me instantly out of my self-pity.

Mike and I were driving to yet another Genie fitting when we saw fire trucks from nearby Dorchester heading into Boston's Back Bay.

"They wouldn't be heading into town if it wasn't bad," Mike said, craning his neck to identify the trucks' company. As he did, my phone started buzzing in my hand with incoming texts: "Is

Mike working today?" "Huge fire on Beacon Street—hope Mike is safe." "Where's Mike? Fire in Back Bay."

Just then Mike got a text from Shana that ran ice water through his veins: *CPR in progress on a firefighter. Beacon Street.*

An apartment-building fire on Beacon Street in Boston's Back Bay, the heart of Mike's firehouse area, had already gone to nine alarms—the highest level of fire emergency.

"You go," I told him as we arrived at the prosthetist's office. "Do what you have to do. I'll call Shana and have her pick me up."

Mike dropped me and raced to his firehouse on Boylston Street only to find it empty; everyone on duty was already at the fire. Mike and other off-duty firefighters from all over the city began to rush to Beacon Street. But it was too late.

As soon as Mike arrived at the scene, he realized the worst: two firefighters from his firehouse had been trapped in the blaze, one had already died from asphyxiation, and the other was in critical condition and on his way to the hospital. One of the men, Lt. Edward Walsh, was from Engine 33, the engine Mike had been working on the day of the bombing, and the other was from Mike's own Ladder 15—Mike Kennedy. Kennedy was the man who had put my leg in the splint, getting me ready for transport in the paddy wagon nearly a year before. Kennedy and Walsh had repeatedly called from their position in the basement of the burning building, pleading for help and alerting other firefighters that they weren't getting any water on the fire because, although the men didn't know it at the time, their hose had burned through. They were trapped behind the blaze in the toxic smoke with no water and no means of escape or rescue.

Before the smoke even cleared, Mike and his fellow firemen knew that they had lost Edward Walsh and Michael Kennedy. Walsh died at the scene; Kennedy was pulled from the basement of the building alive but died soon after from his injuries.

Months after the fire, I listened online to the fire department's audio recording of Kennedy's and Walsh's mayday calls from the basement, and I wept. I wept not only for the men, begging for a rescue that couldn't reach them, but for my Mike and his loss. He had lost friends and colleagues in Iraq, but this was different. This was home. This was his job.

I tried to recall Kennedy's face from that day on Boylston and from when I later thanked him for everything he had done for me, but all I could remember was having seen him at an event the month before and his devilish smile and eyes that lit up with mischief. After meeting Shores at the event, Kennedy had found a quiet moment and pulled the young man aside.

"You got it, kid," Kennedy said. "Scientists have been trying to figure out why some people have it and others don't—that thing that made you turn around and run back toward the trouble. That's something special. You gotta remember that."

Shores didn't know what to say. He had had many people praise his actions, but none had touched him quite like this. Something in Mike Kennedy's urgency, his sincerity, made Shores swallow hard and fight back tears. He reached out and shook Kennedy's hand. "Thank you."

Now Mike Kennedy was gone. That goofy kid with a smile of pure mischief was gone. And so was Ed Walsh, a family man and nine-year veteran of the force, who had approached Mike days after my GoFundMe page went up and handed him two $20 bills. "Here, this is for Roseann's fund. Or maybe just go and buy her lunch or something nice."

Mike could barely talk about it. His natural tendencies toward privacy and controlled emotions took him deep within himself. I struggled to figure out how to help, how to talk about it, even whether to mention it at all. So I didn't.

My immediate reaction to crisis, especially one that involves emotional pain, is to busy myself with as much activity as possible. But Mike's is the opposite. He retreats, reflecting on the loss and carefully processing his emotions. Unfortunately, in this case he wasn't allowed that thoughtful escape because we were suddenly immersed in an endless flurry of funerals, wakes, and events and memorials around the one-year anniversary of the bombing.

The dust had not even begun to settle on the Beacon Street fire before the anniversary activities began and the media started calling, anxious to hear how I was doing and whether I'd like to share my emotions and thoughts about being bombed nearly to kingdom come. Faced with requests to relive and reflect on that day, I did what I always do—I threw myself into action, attending memorials, celebrations, and remembrances. I suppose it was part of my coping mechanism—stay busy. Accept any and all invitations. Try to make the best of what happened to me and have some fun wherever and whenever I can. Plus, all the activity gave me an outlet to talk openly about what had happened, all of which helped me work through the horror.

In the months since the bombing, Shana, Shores, Mike, and I had gathered for dinners together as well as attending the various memorial services, anniversaries, fund-raisers, and memorial walks and runs. While I always enjoyed the events themselves, yet again it was having the four of us together that brought me the most comfort. We just had fun. Well, most of us did. Mike loved being with us but hated being at the memorial events. True to his personality, he tried to avoid it all; he couldn't stand the attention, the questions, and the adoration. He felt that being called a hero, given awards for his actions, celebrating rather than just marking the anniversary, went against everything he had been taught and everything that he believed. His grandfather, father, and uncles had never stood up and beaten their chests in victory. His fellow soldiers in Iraq and Qatar did their jobs and never sought out medals or attention for it. He told me there was a hierarchy to a soldier's wounds. If a guy loses an arm, there's always some other guy who's lost both, and for that guy, there's somebody who was killed. The soldier learns to just keep his head down and move on.

And now, in the aftermath of the bombing and particularly with the ramping up of anniversary activities, I realized that I shared Mike's aversion for those who dwelled on their 4/15 experience rather than picking up the pieces and moving on. It was an odd and unsavory spectacle: people who had been two thousand feet from the bomb were stepping forward, some even trying to claim part of the proceeds from the Boston One Fund, which raised millions of dollars for survivors and families of the deceased. He and I wanted no part of making the anniversary a celebration.

The Campbell, Richard, and Lu families had lost their beautiful son and brother, daughters and sisters, and the Colliers' young son and brother had been ambushed by the bombers while sitting in his cop car at MIT. Many families and lives had been forever altered that day. In the face of *that* real loss and suffering, I kept my pity party to myself. When Mom was told that they had amputated my leg, her first thought had been "Thank God," knowing that they wouldn't have operated on me if I was dead or beyond saving. And as devastating as it has been to lose this leg, it is nothing, *nothing*, compared to what the families of the dead have suffered and will continue to suffer for the rest of their lives.

April 15, 2013, has left me feeling an overwhelming appreciation of life. I am utterly thankful that I am alive and able to walk, even if assisted by my prosthesis. The most significant emotion I experience is gratitude. I can't help but feel how fortunate I am in those who saved my life that day and all the support I have received during my recovery process. What I don't share seems to be the fierce celebration displayed by some who were there that day. They call themselves "survivors" based only on the fact that they were in the vicinity of the bombing. It's difficult for me to find any type of cheerful feeling when I think about the loss of life that occurred around me that day.

Don't get me wrong. I know that many people carry invisible wounds after surviving harrowing events, from brain injuries to PTSD to the emotional toll of being in the middle of a war zone. But when those who were merely there that day present themselves to the media as actual victims of the bombs, equating themselves with those who suffered life-threatening injuries or those who lost limbs and loved ones, I feel my blood pressure begin to rise.

While I was careful to distance myself from the "Marathon Munchausens," I did enjoy getting to know my fellow amputees at the various memorial events and seeing and hearing of their progress as they tried to regain their normal lives. My connection to the other amputees brought with it the unspoken camaraderie of shared loss. We didn't have to explain our sadness, fears, even petty jealousies for the two-leggers who didn't have an ugly, ten-pound albatross tied to their limb. We got each other, easily and completely, and I relaxed just being in their company. As always, Mike wanted none of the gatherings, but he suffered through most of them for me. I didn't want to go alone, and he made sure I didn't have to.

Over the past year, I had also come to love this new family of fellow amputees who understand each other's experiences as no one else could. I also came to respect and honor those affiliated with a list of organizations geared toward supporting amputees: Semper Fi Fund, America's Fund, Challenged Athletes Foundation, Disabled Sports USA, and a surprising number of others. I never realized that there were so many great and important organizations out there.

For the one-year anniversary, the Boston Athletic Association, hoping to reclaim the marathon's exuberance, wanted as many of the survivors as possible to walk the last mile of its 5K, crossing over its famed finish in a celebratory commemoration. The whole five kilometers was too much to consider, but one mile I could definitely handle. Before I even told the BAA whether I'd do it, I called the most important three people and asked if they'd do it with me.

Of course they would.

••••••

After the one-year anniversary events began to die down, Mike and I were able to ease into more of a routine. While the start of our relationship would never, in any universe, be called typical, after a year, we had started to feel more and more like a solid couple, with the usual ups and downs and adjustments of navigating life with another human being in your space, both literally and figuratively. We found ourselves unlikely partners in our neighborhood bar's Trivia Night. I'd like to say I was an equal participant in the game, but that would be a lie. Mike is a history buff and an '8os music junkie. I know pop culture. So while he could reel off the answers to "What were the code names for the five beaches picked by the Allies to invade at Normandy?" (Omaha, Utah, Gold, Juno, and Sword) and "What was President Ulysses S. Grant's birth name?" (Hiram Ulysses Grant), I could name "four movies that starred Reese Witherspoon" (*Sweet Home Alabama*, *Legally Blonde*, *Walk the Line*, and *Election*). I guess I held my own, but I'm glad he was on my team. I don't have to tell you we never won, but we still had fun, even though Mike couldn't understand why I didn't know (or care) which "Whitney Houston single holds the record for the highest one-week single sales?"

"But it's *your* era! How can I know more about '8os music than you?" he chided.

I just gave him the "but *you're* the Whitney Houston fan" look of raised eyebrows over the rim of my wineglass.

"'I Will Always Love You'!" he exclaimed, arms in the air, unable to resist.

While I was settling into this new, wonderful life with this sweet, gentle stranger who loved schmaltzy music and the history of anything and everything, across town scores of attorneys were preparing for the trial of the bombing suspect Dzhokhar Tsarnaev, though it would take nearly a year for the trial to begin.

chapter twelve

THE BROTHERS AND THEIR BOMBS

AS FAR AS I am concerned, the less said about the two Tsarnaev brothers, the better. They took my leg but not my life. They took a lot more from the Richards, the Campbells, the Lus, and the Colliers. I feel sorrow for the ongoing anguish and suffering of those families, and for my fellow survivors who continue to deal with chronic pain and seemingly endless surgeries, but what I feel about the Tsarnaevs is bewilderment. How could anyone hate enough to do what they did? It truly boggles my mind, but it doesn't keep me up at night. What a horrible coincidence that Dzhokhar Tsarnaev, the younger of the two brothers, and Shores were both nineteen- and twenty-year-old (respectively) college kids with their entire lives ahead of them: one chose to kill and the other to save. Tsarnaev had been a popular kid in his progressive high school in Cambridge and had worked part time as a lifeguard at Harvard's Blodgett Pool. He had friends and was intelligent and funny, by all accounts. What happens to someone that causes him to make that kind of horrific choice? *That* is what I'll never understand.

Unlike some of the other amputees, I'm not angry. I knew from early on that rage would do no good, and it certainly wouldn't bring back my leg or those who had died in the blasts. So I focused on moving forward, away from the screams and stink and butchery of the day and toward recovery and my new, adjusted life.

Mike, Shores, and Shana shared my desire to not give Tsarnaev an ounce of undue attention, but in each of them a cold, bitter anger remains. I think it has something to do with their feelings of helplessness at my and the other victims' losses. While I experienced it firsthand and realized I just needed to move on, their experience is a degree removed, and in that degree is a lot of frustration, and even guilt. "What could I have done better?" is a haunting refrain I hear often, and I hear it most from Mike.

"I'm just pissed at those cops for not killing him when they had the chance," he told me, referring to the final shootout and capture of Tsarnaev. "Just to have it done and over with, and not spend the millions upon millions of dollars and thousands of manpower hours on the trial, in addition to the endless media coverage and emotional drain that the survivors will have to go through." Mike had seen how devastating it was for me when *Rolling Stone* put Tsarnaev on its August 2013 cover, almost idolizing him as a teen heartthrob with a sexy "bad boy" photo. I, along with many survivors of that day, will never again buy a single issue of the magazine. Anger aside, we all know that moving on with our lives is the best revenge.

Mike told me he had learned in Iraq that it didn't do any good to care about whether the bad guy lived or died. At the end of the day, after you've found them and dragged them in, they never seem quite as bad as the damage they've done. They end up being some hapless guy with a starving family paid to plant the bomb or sit on a roof with a rifle.

"They're scared shitless," he said. "It's wasted energy to care about them or what happens to them. It's over. It's the same with this punk."

••••••

When it came time for the surviving brother's trial in March of 2015, I didn't want to go. I didn't even want to read or hear about the proceedings. I didn't want to give Tsarnaev, the man who had taken my leg, and the legs and lives of so many others, any more attention.

But something kept nagging at me, and soon I found myself obsessed with every detail of the trial, addicted to all of the tweets, news feeds, and headlines I found. While I probably would never know the real reasons for the Tsarnaev brothers' thirst for the blood of innocent people, I was determined to read every detail, every utterance, every theory. It wouldn't bring peace, and certainly would not bring my leg back, but it would satisfy my need to try to understand. Something about learning everything I could helped to make sense of the senseless and kept my mind busy and the anxiety of living through it all over again at bay.

I was content to never interact with Tsarnaev, but when the federal prosecutor, Assistant US Attorney Steven Mellin, called to ask if I would testify, I knew I had to. If I didn't, and for some crazy reason he was able to walk free or get a reduced sentence on a technicality or through a lack of victim impact statements, I would never forgive myself.

Perhaps the worst part of the entire spectacle was the disgusting appearance of the conspiracy theorists outside the courtroom, calling us "crisis actors" and holding signs proclaiming "EXONERATE! FREE JAHAR!" "FBI ENTRAPMENT = FALSE CONVICTION!" "TSARNAEV IS INNOCENT!" Women came from as far away as Washington State to proclaim their support, even love, for the young bomber. I'm sure that damn *Rolling Stone* cover had something to do with their repulsive passion. I, along with other victims, most wrenchingly those who had lost loved ones, was subjected to their loud, angry ignorance. But I squared my shoulders, looked straight ahead, and walked by them, praying that I would be able to hold my tongue because to respond to their utterly insane belief that it was all a hoax or conspiracy would be pointless. If four dead bodies—three on Boylston Street and Sean Collier's in the MIT shootout—and twenty lost limbs from seventeen people didn't convince them, I certainly wasn't going to.

When it was my turn to face Tsarnaev in the early days of the trial, I was a jumble of nerves as I took the stand. But when the prosecutor asked me to state my name, instead of looking at Steve Mellin, I looked straight at Tsarnaev, less than ten feet away.

Pictures of him taken before the bombing showed an average, clean-cut college kid. But now he had a full, unruly beard; his already thick, dark, curly hair had grown into a huge rat's nest, and he sat low in the chair with his butt pushed all the way to the front edge of the seat, fiddling with a pencil. I couldn't figure out why his defense team hadn't insisted that he shave, get a haircut, and not slouch like a petulant teenager.

Mellin asked me again to state my name. I stared at the man who had caused so much devastation and waited for him to look back. The silence got his attention; he finally looked up at me but then quickly looked back down at his pencil.

"Roseann Sdoia," I said, as slowly and forcefully as my nerves would allow, staring straight at the man Shana had so eloquently labeled "the motherfucker" who had done this. I think something in the quality of my voice got his attention, and he looked up at me again. Unlike the way he had behaved with many of the other victims who'd been on the stand, he held my stare, an insulting smirk on his lips. Absolutely refusing to look away first, I felt a fiery hate burn through me as I stared at the murderer. Suddenly, the court realized what was going on, and Tsarnaev's attorney leaned in front of him, blocking my view and forcing me to look at the prosecutor. As I did, relief flooded in where the hate had been. And to this day, it hasn't come back.

I'd won. He'd taken enough from me; he wasn't going to get another inch of my life or another ounce of my fear.

His defense team never denied that he was guilty of the crime but instead argued that he was the lesser of the perpetrators, that his older brother Tamerlan had been the mastermind who had pulled his impressionable younger brother into the plot. Therefore, they said Dzhokhar deserved a sentence of life in prison rather than the death penalty. As the trial went into deliberations, reporters asked me what I wanted, and I said honestly that what I wanted didn't matter. What was most important was to support the wishes of the families from whom he had taken lives, particularly the Richards, whose son Martin had been killed and whose daughter, Jane, had been maimed by the second bomb. On April 14, 2015, Bill and Denise Richard publicly appealed for the government to take the death penalty off the table through a letter published in the *Boston Globe*. In part it read:

We understand all too well the heinousness and brutality of the crimes committed. We were there. We lived it. The defendant murdered our 8-year-old son, maimed our 7-year-old daughter, and stole part of our soul. We know that the government has its reasons for seeking the death penalty, but the continued pursuit of that punishment could bring years of appeals and prolong reliving the most painful day of our lives. We hope our two remaining children do not have to grow up with the lingering, painful reminder of what the defendant took from them, which years of appeals would undoubtedly bring.

For us, the story of Marathon Monday 2013 should not be defined by the actions or beliefs of the defendant, but by the resiliency of the human spirit and the rallying cries of this great city. We can never replace what was taken from us, but we can continue to get up every morning and fight another day. As long as the defendant is in the spotlight, we have no choice but to live a story told on his terms, not ours. The minute the defendant fades from our newspapers and TV screens is the minute we begin the process of rebuilding our lives and our family.

There is nothing more I could possibly add.

Regardless of the Richards' poignant appeal, a month later, on May 15, 2015, the jury shocked the world by sentencing Tsarnaev to death. As the Richards feared, the case is now in a potentially decades-long appeal process.

Why the Tsarnaev brothers decided to buy BBs, nails, gunpowder, pressure cookers, and remote timers to kill as many innocent people as possible is of little interest to me. And while their names will always be part of Boston Marathon history, I don't want to add any more darkness to that narrative. That's their history. Half of it's dead, and the other half will either join his brother in hell after being put to death by the state, or he will remain in a maximum-security prison for his remaining decades on earth. So be it.

That's all I have to say about them. They took away that day, but we're taking it back.

I am much more invested in having Boston and its wonderful marathon regain the definition of Marathon Monday as an enormous, slightly out-of-control, always fabulous citywide day of celebration. And maybe one day, Marathon Monday will again be my favorite day of the year in Boston.

chapter thirteen

THE LAST HALF MILE

THANK GOD! WAS my first thought on Marathon Monday, 2015. *It's pouring. I don't have to do it.*

Three weeks earlier, I had had lunch with Gregg Edelstein, whom I'd met through the Challenged Athletes Foundation and who was going to run the marathon in my name, wearing the bib I had hoped someday to wear. Over salads and pizza in the North End, I thanked him, wished him well, and tried not to get teary at the awful reality that I may never be able to run Boston. Ever.

I don't believe in tears. Mom's motto has been deeply ingrained in me, and I share her general discomfort, maybe even disdain, for public tears. But the fact that Gregg was going to run the marathon with my bib just plain sucked. I was happy for Gregg, but he didn't need to hear my sadness that I wouldn't be running the marathon myself.

As we finished lunch, he asked if the tricky logistics of downtown Boston on race day and my prosthesis would enable me to watch him finish the race.

His question stopped me in my tracks. Somehow I hadn't realized it before, but if I watched him finish, I would have to stand somewhere on Boylston, in the shadow of where the bombs had exploded, wait for yet another friend in the distance to run toward the finish, and feel the cold steel of the police barricade against my chest as I leaned across it for a better view up the street.

My heart raced, and my stomach flip-flopped. As we sat in that sunny restaurant on Hanover Street, enjoying the first warmth of spring, I knew that returning to Boylston Street on Marathon Monday—any Marathon Monday—was the last thing I wanted to do. But I knew I would. Of course I would. Not only would I go, but I decided right then and there that I would be part of it. If I was going, damnit, this time I wouldn't just be a spectator.

I spoke quickly so that my words would be out there, emblazoned and irrevocable: "I'll be there, and I'll run down Boylston with you to the finish."

But deciding to do it and actually being able to "jump into" the race, and on Boylston, no less, without getting shot by security, prosthesis or no prosthesis, were two different things. A host of agencies might have to be contacted and give their approval, among them the Boston Athletic Association, which organized the race, the Boston Police Department, the Boston Fire Department, Homeland Security, the ATF, and the FBI. (Thankfully, in the end, the race's legendary director, Dave McGillivray, made it happen with a few phone calls.)

Worst of all, Mike didn't like the idea at all, and his concern for my safety began to give me second thoughts. "What if something happens and I can't get to you?"

I looked into his handsome face and saw such deep worry that it broke my heart. "I love you for worrying, but I'll be fine," I said, not at all sure I would be but knowing I was not going to let fear stop me.

•••••••

But, as the good Lord would have it—I awoke to rain on Marathon Monday. Not just rain, but rain that was only going to get worse as the day progressed, developing into pelting, driving sleet, a steady wind out of the east, and temperatures that promised to stay in the 40s. In short, the worst marathon weather possible and the worst I had ever seen in all my years of watching the race.

I don't have to do it! I all but sang out. No one would expect me to follow through with it now. Not on a slippery prosthetic blade. I was off the hook! If I'd had two heels, I would have clicked them in the air.

And yet . . .

Okay, I bargained, *I'll just get ready and see if the worst of the rain lets up. If it does, I'll consider doing it.* McGillivray had worked so hard to get me the clearance to jump the barricades, to say nothing of getting the all clear for Mike to walk through the crowds with a prosthetic leg for which I would trade out my running leg after I crossed the finish line. Backpacks and duffel bags, particularly those large enough to hold a prosthetic leg, are all but banned from large public gatherings, and they're positively forbidden anywhere near Boylston Street on race day. So it took a lot of explaining to the various authorities why an imposing man would be carrying a prosthetic leg (they told us no way they would allow the leg *in* the bag) through the crowded streets of Boston during the marathon. But explain and convince McGillivray did. How could I back out now just because it was raining?

Okay . . . I'll go through the motions and see what happens. Besides, the rain would keep the spectators at bay: Boylston Street wouldn't be as crazy crowded as it usually is for the marathon. At least I had that going for me.

Suddenly, all of my inner debate about whether to run or not was moot. It was time. One of Mike's coworkers from the Boylston firehouse, Timmy Freda, who had also been on Boylston Street helping save survivors two years before, walked me to the barricade and spoke to a cop on the inside of the police line, and the two men moved the fence aside so I could stand on Boylston and wait for Gregg. Mike disappeared into the crowd toward the finish line with Genie held high above his head, and I stood in the torrential rain watching runners come toward me.

How in hell did this happen? It was still raining, *hard*, I was already wet, and yet there I was, about to jog down Boylston Street to the finish of the Boston Marathon.

And I did.

Gregg soon appeared around the corner of Hereford, beaming and wrapping me in a huge hug, and we started off. Then something happened. In all of the planning and worrying about actually running the last half mile, I hadn't had time to really think about what, if any, reaction the crowd might have. But as we trotted away from the barricade and into the middle of the street and the notoriously, wondrously exuberant crowds on Boylston saw me, something happened. Something magical. Having seen the impenetrable police barricades part for me to slip through, those near the breach noticed and, like a game of telephone tag, I started to hear word spread: "She's jumping in!"

Crossing the finish line after running the last ½ mile of the 2015 Boston Marathon with Greg Edelstein, Challenged Athlete Volunteer and my friend.

"That's *her*."

"Oh, my God, she's going to run!"

"Look! She's one of the survivors!"

"She's RUNNING!"

"Look at HER! She's going for it!"

They went wild. It was beyond cheers—it was a roar. A mass exultation. A solid wall of screams, of whistles, of cheers, of hoots and hollers and hoorays. They might not know my name, but they knew my story, and the stories of my fellow survivors.

It was as if I and my prosthesis, drenched in the rain, running in the Boston Marathon, personified something real and vital about taking back our race and redeeming our city. It was as if the entire crowd, the entire city, was yelling a collective "ENOUGH! THIS IS OUR RACE, THIS IS OUR TOWN, AND YOU WILL NOT TAKE IT FROM US!"

Two years before, we had had our favorite day destroyed, our city brought to its knees, and our loved ones murdered in front of our eyes. But not today. Today, two years later, I and the entire city of Boston took it back. As I ran on that wet, miserable, magical day, as I looked around me and saw pride in the overjoyed faces, I realized we were all taking back our race. And our city.

Slowly, Gregg and I continued down the slick pavement, my mascara in black streaks down my face, both from the rain and from my own tears, and my hair slick to my head. But I only felt a wondrous sort of joy that I was feeling the simple pleasure of the weather again. In the two years since the bombing, first my crutches and then my prosthesis had almost imprisoned me against the weather—snow, sleet, rain, wind, and ice were all too treacherous now. So I had come to avoid anything but dry and calm. But here I was, struggling not to fall on each crosswalk's slippery white paint, soaked to the skin, feeling the rain course down my head, into my eyes, and yes, into my prosthesis—but it felt like heaven. It felt normal. I, like everybody else, was wet in the rain.

Soon Gregg and I passed the green mailbox where my right leg had been torn from my body and where Martin Richard's and Lingzi Lu's lives had drained into the bricks. I said a silent prayer and kept moving. Then we passed where Krystle Campbell had been standing, cheering on her friend, when the first bomb had exploded at her feet. Again I said a silent prayer and kept moving.

As I approached the finish line, I stopped and took one last look back up Boylston Street. All of the mixed emotions and memories it contained were behind me.

Then I turned and saw Mike, weaving through the crowds toward me, carrying Genie high above his head to protect it from the dazed and exhausted finishers bumping into him. Shores was close behind him, soaked to the skin and beaming. Shana was watching from a police monitoring station high above the finish line, cheering like a crazy woman.

I took a deep breath, and then, finally, walked across the finish line and toward the people who got me there.

November 2014—The Perfect Strangers at a UMass–Lowell vs. Northeastern hockey game.

Courtesy of Mark Duffy

MOVING ON

AS THESE PAGES go to press, it's been more than five years since April 15, 2013, and my life has changed in every conceivable way—physically, professionally, and, of course, personally. I went from life on two legs to learning how to walk and live on one. I went from being a vice president of a real estate firm to being a motivational public speaker and writer. I went from being a single woman who met up with a group of my friends for Sunday brunches to finding an incredible husband in Mike. And now Shores and Shana come to the home where we live together for pizza and beer. I still see my girlfriends as much as time will allow, but more and more I find myself content to stay in and spend the evening with just us four. My perfect strangers.

Physically, I'm continuing to heal, though I still hit some of the bumps in the road that most amputees deal with—skin irritation from the liner, soreness, difficulty with the fit of the prosthesis. When I go to the doctor, unless I'm seeing a specialist in amputee health, they often can't relate and offer solutions that aren't really viable for an amputee. So I've gotten creative, coming up with some remedies on my own, like using ointment and powder on my residual limb to create a barrier and prevent skin irritation. And I've become a bit less active over the past few years. Maybe it's because it's just harder now to be as active as I used to be, or maybe it's because I'm happier and more settled in my lifestyle, but I'm steadily regaining my motivation, and I have a strong commitment to regaining my pre-2013 active lifestyle.

I still struggle with attending outdoor events with large crowds—I suspect this will always be the case to some extent. As I write this, Boston is preparing for the Red Sox championship parade to celebrate their World Series win. If this was happening prior to 2013, I'd definitely be in the crowd, cheering with my friends and family. But this year I'm staying home. It's too uncontained, and there are too many open targets. This is how I assess events with large crowds these days. When a friend asks me to go to a concert or large event, my mind runs through a series of questions: How many people will be there? Is there a police presence? Will I feel safe?

I think it's hard for people who haven't gone through an amputation to understand this caution. I and the other survivors are still interviewed periodically about the experience and our recovery, and those who interview us seem so positive. The public can see that we're healing and walking, and it makes them feel better, I think, to imagine that our lives are back to normal. But what is normal? When I stand up from the kitchen table, my foot can get stuck under the table leg. I can't just jump out of bed, throw on shoes, and run out the door. Every step, every activity is calculated. I have to think five steps ahead of whatever

I'm doing in any given moment so I'll be prepared and not slow down the rest of the world (or land on my butt!).

My professional life continues to change. I do book signings, motivational speaking, and volunteer mentoring for new amputees. As long as people continue to ask me to share my story, I will do so. Every person who approaches me and tells me how our story has helped them in some way reminds me that I'm on the right path. Meeting all the people I have encountered along the way of sharing my story has been nothing short of amazing.

I will be forever indebted to all of the organizations and individuals that helped make this process a bit easier—there are too many to name here. I can't imagine going through an amputation and recovery without the help that I received from each and every one of them. It has become a mission to pay it forward whenever possible.

Over these last four years I have been asked, "How did you cope with losing a leg?" The answer is very simple: I just kept going, and I moved on. We all did. And I think that's at the core of why we four have become so bonded together: We all had the same reaction to the tragedy and the terror. Yes, we found ourselves in the middle of this catastrophic event, but we never allowed it to define us or to become who we are or who we are going to be. While we have been deeply affected by what happened on April 15, 2013, we are still, at our cores, the same people we were before the bombs went off—only now we're better because we each have the love, respect, and care of the other three. Our gatherings are always defined by the easy fun and laughter of simply being in each other's presence.

We never forget that as horrific and devastating as the bombings were, they pale in comparison to other terrorist attacks, both here and around the world. Everywhere, it seems, innocent lives are lost or maimed by a handful, sometimes only one or two, who have decided that their view of the world is the only view and that those who think and believe differently should die. Sometimes killing isn't enough, and the terrorists make a point of inflicting prolonged torture, kidnapping, and hostage-taking and posting gruesome online executions. As much as I am haunted by what happened to me on Boylston Street, it truly isn't even on the same radar screen as what untold others have suffered at the hands of hate.

While we have all done our best to move on, a cold sadness and fear do linger in my heart because I always expect it to happen again, somewhere, sometime. But until then, I will live life, feel love, and express gratitude for each and every day.

In April 2015, a few months before his graduation, Shores Salter was honored by his soon-to-be alma mater, Northeastern University, when it established the first annual Shores C. Salter Award for Outstanding Citizenship. The citation noted Shores's "exceptional courage and compassion, going above and beyond to help" the wounded in the bombing. The award designates a student who has made "an outstanding contribution to our local or global community through service, leadership and dedication" and has since been presented to three students who have followed in Shores's footsteps. At the ceremony, I told the audience that I would always be grateful for his heroism that day but that I was even more thankful for what came later: his friendship. A rare young man and an old soul, Shores makes me smile every time he comes through the door with a huge grin on his face, a bottle of wine in his hand to have with dinner, and an enveloping hug for everyone in the room. For his part, Shores accepted the award with a simple "Thank you," waved at his family and friends, and sat down. Once again, it wasn't about him.

After graduating in May 2015 with a degree in chemistry, Shores applied to and was accepted into the one-year master's degree program at Northeastern to study chemical biology and chemistry. After watching his mother undergo the diagnosis and treatment of breast cancer, his hope was to somehow be a part of eradicating the ruin that cancer inflicts on the human body. And it still weighs in the back of his mind. In the spring of 2016, when we finally identified and contacted the elusive doctor who had held my hand on Boylston Street, Shores had coffee with him near Northeastern. Like Mike Kennedy, Dr. Collin Stultz told Shores that what he has can't be taught.

"Fight or flight—all humans are hard-wired to either panic and run or stay calm and hold their ground. Most are the former. You are the latter," Stultz told him. He also told him that he saved my life that day. "Without that tourniquet, she could absolutely have died. Have you thought of becoming a doctor?"

He hadn't, but Stultz planted a seed, and Shores has thought about it since then. Shores completed graduate school and is working for a medical device company. He hopes that his job will take him out of Massachusetts for a bit, as he has always lived here. I hope he gets everything he wants, but I will miss him.

In 2017, Shores ran the Boston Marathon for the Heather Abbott Foundation, which provides customized prostheses for people who have lost limbs due to traumatic circumstances. I've never been so proud of him or touched by his continued support and love.

In the months after the bombing, Shana took stock of her life and reflected on just how close she felt she had come to losing it. She has taken a hard look at her career to decide how to carve out more personal time and experience less danger. After being the top-scoring female on her exam, she has been promoted to sergeant, and she is still working in Boston. On Labor Day of 2017, Shana tied the knot with her longtime live-in girlfriend, Sarah. They have a dog, Monkey, and recently decided to adopt a kitten, Chainsaw.

My family is still the weird amalgam of tenderness and tension, but we're learning. It's how we interact—it's all we know, and I wouldn't have it any other way. Dad and I have shared some wonderful moments in the past couple of years over our gluten-free meals (gluten allergies are largely hereditary, so thanks for that, Dad!). He was always physically demonstrative, but since the bombing, he has greeted me, and now Mike, with even bigger hugs than before. Writing the book has brought me and my father closer together. It has opened a dialogue between us that I'm incredibly grateful for.

Mom, on the other hand, is still Mom. She still won't let me properly hug her. In fact, several months after the bombing, when life was getting back to some semblance of normalcy, Mom came over to have dinner with us, and Mike stood to give her a big hug when she came through the front door. As he approached her, she straight-armed him.

"We're done with all the hugging, right?"

Mike backed away, slightly taken aback but not hurt. He too had come to know my mother's limitations, and the constant bear hugs were clearly among them.

My parents' values, lessons, and guidance made me who I was on April 15, 2013, and who I am today. It is because of them that I survived and continue to thrive.

As Mike and I got further from April 15, 2013, we grew closer and closer. Over the months and then years, we have talked less about the past as the future has become our focus. As I write this, Mike and I have just celebrated the one-year anniversary of our wedding. We got engaged on December 4, 2016, on Nantucket at the Whaling Museum. It was the annual Christmas Stroll, held every year during the first weekend of December. I'd never been—it's an undeniably romantic event, and I had never had anyone particularly special to go with. We booked a room at one of the local hotels (one that allows pets, of course!), and Sal joined us. We spent the first evening bouncing from one local shop to another, and when we grew tired, we sat down on the beautiful wraparound porch at the Nantucket Hotel for a drink. I thought it would be a relaxing evening, sitting on the porch by a firepit with a warm blanket. Little did I know he had planned to propose earlier—when we first arrived on the island, he asked if we could go for a walk on the beach to see the sunset. But I performed my regular "amputee assessment" and told him I wasn't feeling up for a walk of that distance or for dealing with the sand in my prosthetic foot. A missed opportunity! But another one was around the corner. While I was in the bathroom, Mike ended up chatting with Sandi, who worked at the Whaling Museum, and told her about his plan to propose. She was excited about helping him out. When I returned, we all began talking, and Sandi offered to give us a private tour on Sunday before we left the island. It sounded like a great way to end our trip, so we made plans to meet her there the next morning.

Around 10 a.m., Sandi brought us up to the empty observation deck. As I looked out at the harbor, commenting on how beautiful it was, I noticed that Mike had wandered over to a corner with Sal. I heard a tiny jingling sound and saw Mike bending over, playing with Sal's collar. "Have you seen Sal's new dog tags?" he asked. I thought it was an odd question—we hadn't gotten him new tags. "Look at them," he said. As I bent down, I saw that there were three small metal tags. They read (in Sal's "voice"), in order:

"Uhh, he wants to know . . ."

"If uh, you'll say YES?"

"I love you, Mike—(+Sal)."

We married on October 21, 2017, a sunny and cool New England fall day. We wanted the day to be a celebration and to be meaningful and were privileged to have Matt Seigel, the local host of the Boston radio program *Matty in the Morning*, officiate at the ceremony, which took place just outside the Kingman Yacht Club in Pocasset, Massachusetts. Matt, along with his wife, has always been incredibly supportive of us and other survivors, so it just felt right to have him there.

Everyone says to take a minute, step back, and take the day in. I did my best, but it still went by in a flash, and I would love the opportunity to relive every minute of it. Aside from not being able to invite so many who mean so much to us, it was all that I could have wanted and then some. We were surrounded by all the people we love, and there was so much positive energy all night. The dance floor was never empty, and Mike even made a surprise appearance onstage with the band, adding backup vocals to one of his favorite songs, "Africa" by TOTO.

We honeymooned in Riviera Maya, Mexico, for eight days. Believe it or not, it was the first time Mike and I had gone away by ourselves with no agenda other than to be together. It was completely magical.

We're back home now, and now back to reality. I've had a second surgery on my right ear to remove a cholesteatoma, a cyst in the middle ear, most likely caused by the implosion of my eardrum when the bomb exploded. While I was recovering and passing time, we decided it was a good idea to add a new puppy, Lou, to the family. At times it seems as if he drives Sal crazy by constantly following his older brother around, but the two genuinely love each other. Although their personalities couldn't be more different, it's fun to watch them interact. They both put smiles on our faces, especially when we take them to run on the beach or around a cranberry bog on the cape.

Mike still works at the same Boylston Street firehouse. He still enjoys the busy call volume that goes with working at a firehouse in that part of the city, and he serves alongside the same group of guys that he has worked with for years.

In 2018, Mike chose to run the Boston Marathon. When Mike is asked about his experience, he is quick to correct the term "run" with a more appropriate "shuffle." Mike wasn't very excited about running (or shuffling) along the course at all, especially in the monsoonlike conditions of that 2018 race day. But he loved being on a small team of firefighters who ran to honor Ed Walsh, one of their friends who had perished in the 2014 Beacon Street fire. Their race raised funds for the Ed Walsh Foundation, which supports Boston families in need. Mike stuck with it for all 26.2 miles, taking the right on Hereford and then the left on Boylston Street. I watched him turn the corner, so proud of him. I was also profoundly touched to be able to "run" with him over the freshly painted blue-and-yellow finish line as he finished. (He credits his success to a great iPod playlist and chowing down on some pizza from a friend at mile 19.)

Like every couple, Mike and I still have our moments, little squabbles that pepper our days, mostly due to my being perpetually late. But these challenging moments are few and brief and are part of the mosaic of any good relationship. As with everything else, we move on. And it's all good. Really good. Life is still very busy for both of us but is becoming a bit more routine. And he continues to make me feel safe by having him by my side, and with every adventure our life together becomes more fun. We don't take as many scenic car rides as we did in the past, but we still squeeze them in every so often. Of course, Mike's musical interests have remained the same, so we can always agree on a Bruce Springsteen and Billy Joel mix. But mostly we love just being home in Boston, finding new restaurants, enjoying (or mocking) the latest movies, and spending as much time as possible with family and friends. He never ceases to amaze me with his kindness, making sure I have water in the car on road trips, buying me cards and flowers just because, and constantly texting me pictures or comments that make me laugh out loud. And we always sign off our phone calls with a simple "I love you."

One question that I am frequently asked is would I give it all back if I could get my leg back? In the beginning, I didn't think I could honestly answer that question. It was tough for me to think about whether I would rather have my leg or keep these three strangers in my life. Over the last five years, though, time has helped me see that life does go on. I've always said I had a good life before, and I wanted to continue that good life after the bombing. The friends that I've made since that fateful day have certainly made this difficult situation that much more livable. We have done that together, living the life I had before. I try to enjoy the good, the bad, and the ugly—that is what living is all about. Things are definitely not as easy as they were in the past, but I would never give up anything that I have done or any of the people who have become part of our lives these past five years. We are continually astonished at how many good people are out there in the world, so *many* more than the bad. Family, friends, and complete strangers who have become the fabric of our lives.

As the saying goes, life is good. In fact, I can't imagine it any other way.

RESOURCES:
FOR THOSE NOT AS "LUCKY" AS I WAS

Almost immediately after the blast on April 15, 2013, I became aware of just how lucky I was. An entire city, indeed a nation and world, became my support system, from having a stranger step forward to save my life on Boylston Street to receiving the best medical care imaginable to financial assistance to rare, if not unheard-of, insurance coverage to a bedside visit from the president of the United States, who personally guaranteed that I wouldn't be alone in regaining my life.

While learning that I have been incredibly fortunate, I have also come to realize just how forgotten and even ignored tens of thousands of other amputees are—those who lose a leg to diabetes or infection or return from our wars in Iraq and Afghanistan without their arms and legs or are maimed by catastrophic car and industrial accidents. All too many of those people suffer not only the loss of one or more limbs but also the added insult to injury of being treated like bothersome burdens by the health care system and as chattel by their insurance companies, when they have insurance at all. Many don't, and are therefore condemned to life without a second arm or to one in a wheelchair, unable to afford a five-figure prosthesis.

Many of those less fortunate than I have reached out to me, asking for guidance and advice on resources, available support groups and foundations, and referrals to advocates in and for the disabled community.

Here are some humble thoughts for anyone who might be going through something similar, gained through my own experience but not meant to be scripture, only suggestions.

- The loss of a limb is a kind of death, and just as with death, there are five stages in the process: Denial, Anger, Bargaining, Depression, and, finally, Acceptance. That last one is the most important.
- Grieve for the limb: it was worth it.
- If you feel that you need to talk to somebody, find a good therapist.
- If you have time, try to find a prosthetist *before* the amputation operation. Here are five questions I have found invaluable. (Others can be found on my website, http://robostrong.com.)

1. How long will it take from the first fitting to when I receive my prosthesis?
2. How long will it take me to be seen should I have a problem?
3. What type of coverage/support is there for weekends, the prosthetist's vacation, or if I am out of town and need an adjustment?
4. Do you give your patients your cell-phone number for an emergency?
5. When my leg needs to go into the "shop" for a "tune-up," will I get a comparable loaner leg?

- Again, if you have warning of your amputation, meet with your surgeon and your prosthetist *before* the operation and ask and learn everything you can about life with your changed limb.
- Interview as many prosthetists as you can until you find the company *and* individual with whom you'll feel comfortable working. As I said earlier in the book, besides their life partner, two people know a female amputee most intimately—their gynecologist and their prosthetist. So choose wisely.
- Within the first twelve to twenty-four months, your limb will change quite frequently, which in turn will make your prosthesis fit differently, sometimes even from day to day. Keep a diary of your activity and what you have eaten, both of which will make your limb fluctuate.
- Ask your prosthetist any and all questions; no question is stupid or too small.
- Do your research, starting with the Amputee Coalition (http://www.amputee-coalition.org). They can help with finances, prosthetic equipment, classes, etc.
- You are your own best advocate. You need to speak up if things are not fitting right or even if you don't like the look of something. If you don't fix it, you won't wear it!
- Fight for what you need with your insurance company; a prosthesis is *not* a luxury.
- Don't be afraid or intimidated if your prosthetist is no longer a "good fit." You have every right to move on.

Here is a list of additional organizations that might be helpful:

- Challenged Athletes Foundation: www.challengedathletes .org

- Wiggle Your Toes: www.wiggleyourtoes.org
- Claddagh Fund: www.claddaghfund.org
- The Greg Hill Foundation: www.thegreghillfoundation.org
- Limbs for Life Foundation: www.limbsforlife.org
- 50 Legs: www.50legs.org
- A Leg Forever Foundation: www.alegforever.com
- The Heather Abbott Foundation: www.heatherabbottfoundation.org

Also, there are many local, national, and international service organizations, some more active than others, depending on where you live. You could contact any of these and ask what resources might be available:

Lions Club: www.lionsclubs.org
Rotary: www.rotary.org
Benevolent and Protective Order of Elks: www.elks.org
Shriners: www.shrinershq.org
Knights of Columbus: www.kofc.org

Finally, if you have any other questions or concerns, please don't hesitate to contact me at roseann@robostrong.com.

ACKNOWLEDGMENTS

To start, I would like to thank my mother and father for being there for me every step of the way. Reflecting on the past in order to write it down here was not the easiest task for any of us, but please know how much I love you both. I am who I am today and have succeeded in life, before and after April 15, 2013, because of you.

Mom and Donald, Dad and Lennie, Gia and Patrick, Jane, Jessica, Bridget, Auntie Paula, Grandma Sara (who lived long enough to witness the horror inflicted on her granddaughter but sadly left us before she could read in these pages how it all turned out), and lastly Uncle Billy and Auntie Elaine: you all are what motivated me to stay alive that day. Without you, I don't know where I would be today. (And on a poignant note, I am thankful that Gramma Rose was not here to witness any of the tragedy.)

The courage of those who helped me and the other victims that day can never be forgotten. Whether it was Boston police, Boston firefighters, EMS, doctors, nurses, other first responders, and just everyday civilians—their strength and selfless acts will remain with me forever. Without their quick action, I would not be alive to write this story. All I can say is thank you for what you did that day. Firefighters, police, and first responders get up every morning in order to help keep strangers safe and often alive: thank you for what you do every day, and what you did that day. What happened on "4/15" was above and beyond your call of duty, even if you think you were "just doing your job." I will never believe anything else.

Although it was a catastrophic event, my life has been blessed by those who were ready and waiting at Massachusetts General Hospital to save the survivors in their care. Dr. David King: thank you for keeping me alive and putting me back together. Thank you, as well, for all your years of service to our country, not only here, but on the front lines in Iraq and Afghanistan. I truly believe I had a faster road to recovery because of your incomparable battlefield experience working on our men and women in uniform as well as untold thousands in earthquake-torn Haiti. To the staff in the MGH emergency room, operating room, and ICU: thank you for taking such good and gentle care of me. You made me feel safe and secure. To the team at Spaulding Rehabilitation Hospital: I think of you often and am grateful for all that you do to help people get back to their normal way of life, even if it is a new normal. I will always feel a special bond with all of those whom I came into contact with because of their hard work and dedication to helping strangers get well again. Thanks also to Justin Mederios, a personal trainer at Boston Sports Club in West Newton, for donating his time to learning how to work with an amputee and helping me with my "life after" Spaulding. And that is just the short list. There were many more people who helped me along the way whose names and faces are a blur, but know that you're not forgotten.

I will forever be indebted to the partners and my coworkers at National Development, along with many vendors and clients with whom I worked over the years. After the bombing, everyone stepped in—helping cover my job, relieving much physical and mental stress as I struggled to regain a sense of well-being, and finally by making sure my transition home was smooth. The time and support you gave helped me evaluate my new life and put me at ease, reducing a lot of pressure as I tried to figure things out.

I have also received enormous support from elementary, middle, and high school and college friends and coworkers who have become friends: you all pushed me over that recovery "hump." Knowing what a good life I had had before 4/15 with all of you kept me motivated and focused on how I wanted to regain that same good life in the future.

To all of you who helped set up my GoFundMe account as well as the Lotsa Helping Hands schedule, there are no words that I can use other than THANK YOU for jumping into action. The immediate setup of the fund has given me peace of mind, knowing that I will be able to afford health care and the best prostheses for years to come. Lotsa Helping Hands made me less anxious about my return home because I knew I would not be left alone to fend for myself in those early days and nights in my apartment. To all the others who were at the hospital in what seemed like seconds and were thinking ahead of the game, I will forever be grateful, as God only knows where my car would have been towed or what would have happened to Nellie and Missy . . . and, oh, the gluten-free whoopie pies. And to those of you who came endlessly to visit, your company, entertainment, and pure friendship kept my positive attitude intact. My recovery would have been a lot more lonely and a lot less fun without you. To those of you who had to travel long distances, thank you.

I am truly blessed with all those whom I have had in my life over the years.

Then there are those whom I do not know personally. To start, thank you to the residents of my hometown of Dracut, Massachusetts, to those where I live now in the North End of Boston, and of course to everyone around the world who let all of us survivors know we were not going through this alone. From near or far, in person, through e-mails and letters or donations, it all meant more than you will ever know. You will always have my sincerest gratitude.

Thank you to those celebrities who took time to connect with us. The mere fact of your visits helped lift our spirits, putting a smile on our faces at a time of need.

Over the past three-plus years, I have been fortunate to meet many courageous and noble people who have made it their mission to help those less fortunate or in need through organizations such as the Challenged Athletes Foundation, Disabled Sports USA, Semper Fi / America's Fund, Spread the Love Foundation, NEADS (National Education for Assistance Dog Services), Operation Warrior Wishes, the Claddagh Foundation, Wiggle Your Toes, and many others. Your dedication to such work is priceless to those in need.

To Megan, Sabrina, Jenna, and Alissa, who were with me enjoying that beautiful afternoon in front of Forum, thinking our only concern was whether we'd miss our friends running past without getting a photo with them—we will forever have this true bond. In an instant, our favorite day turned into our worst. There is no way to express what happened and what it meant for me to know you are all alive. I had feared the worst. While I am sorry we went through this, I am so grateful I didn't go through it alone. I went through it with you, and now, years later, I think about you all the time.

Not knowing anything about this book-writing process, I am sure I have driven both my agent, Katherine Flynn of Kneerim and Williams Agency, and writer, Jennifer Jordan, a little crazy from time to time. I want to apologize and thank you at the same time. Your dedication and belief in this story have helped me put the pen to paper and made it what it is today. It is a book I am proud to have my name on. Thank you for the untold hours spent interviewing family and friends, coworkers and hospital workers, and many others who were involved. Thank you for listening to me rant and occasionally having to talk me off the ledge. It has been an overwhelming experience, but I am glad that both of you were there to help me through it. This includes the endless help from PublicAffairs. To my editor, Colleen Lawrie, thank you for your insights and bringing all of our stories into one. Kristina, Lindsay, Miguel, and Jaime, your help on getting our story out there is much appreciated. You have all helped make this process much easier and smoother.

I would be remiss if I didn't mention those who were and have been part of my moving forward in the days, months, and years after the bombings, including those at the FBI and the US Attorney's Office and my prosthetists at Next Step and now Medical Center Orthotics and Prosthetics. It truly has taken a small village to get me to where I am today; with that, I say thank you.

Lastly but most importantly, thank you to Shores, Shana, and my love, Mike. First, thank you for agreeing to be part of this book. It is truly as much your book as it is mine. I know it has been difficult opening up and talking about such private moments. And the same goes to your families for being willing to be part of this process and sharing their perspectives with real honesty and emotion. We experienced a devastating tragedy but have come through to the other side. You have been there from the blast right up to today. Our visits, friendship, and my and Mike's relationship are things no one will ever be able to replace. You have all made me feel secure, safe, and indestructible. I cherish the times that we spend together. I can't even remember what my life was like in the days before I had you! I hope you have all found this story to be more of a happy-ending experience than a burdensome one. At least that has been my intention in sharing our story of friendship and love.

I love you, Mike. There are so many things that I am thankful for because of you. Thank you for being the kind, caring, giving, and loving person you are. You have served our country, helping to protect our freedom, and now you serve on the Boston Fire Department, protecting Boston's citizens. Your concern for others is what draws me to you, along with your quiet yet quick sense of humor. I love how you have taught me to appreciate pizza. Most importantly, you always keep me guessing *and* laughing. And now I am thankful that we have Sal in our lives. I look forward to experiencing a fun and loving future with both of you!

I hope I haven't left anyone out. But if I have, please know that I have endless gratitude for all of you and for this life you helped save, rebuild, and rejuvenate.

Much love to all!

Roseann

Roseann Sdoia is a public speaker and advocate for amputees. She is considering one day running the entire 26.2-mile Boston Marathon. In November 2014, she completed her first 5K race. *Perfect Strangers* is her first book.

Photograph by Julie Schoening

Jennifer Jordan is an author, filmmaker, and journalist. Both of her previous books, *Savage Summit* and *Last Man on the Mountain*, won the National Outdoor Book Award. She also produced several documentaries, including *Kick Like a Girl* and *3,000 Cups of Tea: Investigating the Rise and Ruin of Greg Mortenson*.

Photograph by Jeff Rhoads

PublicAffairs is a publishing house founded in 1997. It is a tribute to the standards, values, and flair of three persons who have served as mentors to countless reporters, writers, editors, and book people of all kinds, including me.

I. F. STONE, proprietor of *I. F. Stone's Weekly*, combined a commitment to the First Amendment with entrepreneurial zeal and reporting skill and became one of the great independent journalists in American history. At the age of eighty, Izzy published *The Trial of Socrates*, which was a national bestseller. He wrote the book after he taught himself ancient Greek.

BENJAMIN C. BRADLEE was for nearly thirty years the charismatic editorial leader of *The Washington Post*. It was Ben who gave the *Post* the range and courage to pursue such historic issues as Watergate. He supported his reporters with a tenacity that made them fearless and it is no accident that so many became authors of influential, best-selling books.

ROBERT L. BERNSTEIN, the chief executive of Random House for more than a quarter century, guided one of the nation's premier publishing houses. Bob was personally responsible for many books of political dissent and argument that challenged tyranny around the globe. He is also the founder and longtime chair of Human Rights Watch, one of the most respected human rights organizations in the world.

. . .

For fifty years, the banner of Public Affairs Press was carried by its owner Morris B. Schnapper, who published Gandhi, Nasser, Toynbee, Truman, and about 1,500 other authors. In 1983, Schnapper was described by *The Washington Post* as "a redoubtable gadfly." His legacy will endure in the books to come.

Peter Osnos, *Founder*